CDL MINDED ACCOUNTING

THE CLUTTER PROOF SYSTEM TO CONTROLLING YOUR FINANCES IN YOUR TRANSPORTATION AND TRUCKING BUSINESS

JOE RYDER

Cover Designer: Kenneth Ryan Monteclaro
Interior Design by FormattedBooks.com

TABLE OF CONTENTS

CDL Business Productivity GAME PLAN

Entrepreneurs Guide to Quick Start your Business to the Next Level

Thank you! Here's a Free Gift! For You :)

As a special thanks from me to you, you'll receive:

- ❏ 3 Powerful Elements of Productivity in your Business
- ❏ 5 Simple Strategies to Mastering Productivity in your Business
- ❏ The Highest Quality of Productivity Charts
- ❏ Valuable Resources that you Must Know and much more!

To receive your Free copy of the CDL Business Productivity GAME PLAN, you can go to my website at:

cdlforlife.com/cdl-business-resources

<u>SCAN ME</u>
(For your Free Business Game Plan)

<u>SCAN ME</u>
(If you want my Books for Free)

Also If you would like to get my books for Free and before anyone else, go to my website at:

cdlforlife.com/cdl-business-resources

INTRODUCTION

After many months of preparation, fundraising, and putting your plans into motion, you're ready to launch your trucking or transportation business. You know all the ins and outs of how to manage your employees, find customers, market your new company, and fulfill orders. There's just one little thing you forgot: finances!

Finance can be a tricky subject for regular life, and it only gets more complex when the health of your business is dependent on your accounting skills. If you don't have a lot of experience overseeing the accounting needs of a company, you can fall into common pitfalls such as overspending in unimportant areas, underfunding critical ones, and failing to save for the future. Keeping track of financial documents can also be a pain if you don't start off on the right foot. Poor accounting management can become a big problem for your business very quickly, and if financial problems persist, they can spell ruin before you've even fully gotten off the ground.

If you try to run your business without any knowledge of accounting, you're going to experience a lot of problems very quickly. While you can make things easier on yourself by hiring an accountant, they might not understand what it means to work in the commercial trucking industry, nor will they know the specific needs of your company like you do. Letting someone else control the company finances without any input from you means you're not involved or knowledgeable enough to assist in the decision-making process, and it increases your risk of being defrauded or misled. Even if you do end up outsourcing financial matters, it's still important for you to understand these issues as a business owner so you can evaluate how well your company is doing and use this information to make informed decisions.

Understanding the commercial driver's license (CDL) industry and how to succeed in it is only half the battle. Taking time to learn about smart financial moves will give you a leg up over your competitors and start you down the road to success. Luckily, understanding business finances doesn't have to be a difficult task. With the right guide, it's actually very simple to avoid common mistakes that most people make, which would otherwise prevent you from setting up your business for future success.

CDL Minded Accounting is exactly that guide. Inside, you'll learn the basics of how to manage your company's finances, including how to navigate taxes, setting yourself up as an LLC, and ensuring you're doing everything by the book. As you read, you'll develop an understanding of various bookkeeping terms. You'll also learn about the one-of-a- kind, clutter-proof system for accounting that allows you to keep track of the many different variables in play when dealing with business finances, such as record keeping, payroll, and cost management.

We understand how to keep a business running because we've been in the trucking industry for over 25 years. We know what it takes to build a trucking business from the ground up, and we want to help you do the same so financial barriers won't hold you back from pursuing your dreams. Entrepreneurship is often full of uncertainty, but you can learn and apply your newfound knowledge about money matters in order to keep the financial risks of starting your own business in check.

You don't need a degree in economics to run your trucking company. With CDL-minded accounting and the clutter-proof system, you'll have no trouble leading the way to achieve financial freedom and security with your new business.

CHAPTER 1

Getting Registered

B efore you can start operating as a trucking company, you'll need to register your business and make sure you have any necessary permits. It might feel a little like you're jumping through hoops, but it's important to get this step right. Registering ensures that your company is recognized as a legitimate, legal business and that all operations are above board. It can be tricky to figure out exactly what you need to operate legally, but it's worth it for the certainty that you won't be hit with a lawsuit or a huge fine sometime down the road for not being properly registered.

Thankfully, when you go through all the right channels, it's not too difficult to get all the necessary permits and licenses if you know what you're doing. In this chapter, we'll look at the various legal requirements for running a trucking business, as well as how you can ensure you're complying with the relevant federal, state, and local laws in your area. We'll also cover tax-related subjects like setting up an LLC and getting registered for tax season so you can take advantage of all the tax deductions and breaks for small business owners covered in Chapter 6.

Acquiring Licenses and Permits

Trucking is a pretty regulated industry with a lot of strict standards, and for good reason. An unlicensed driver who hasn't passed a road test might pose a higher risk of getting into an accident and hurting themselves and others. Not going through the proper channels and getting the right permits can be disastrous. Therefore, you'll need to acquire various permits and licenses before your business is fully operational.

Some of the legal documents you'll need when you're getting started include commercial driver's licenses, Department of Transportation and Motor Carrier Authority numbers, a unified carrier registration, an International Registration Plan tag, an International Fuel Tax Agreement decal, and the relevant local permits for oversize vehicles. You'll also need to fill out the BOC-3 form, and certain businesses will also need a Standard Carrier Alpha Code.

Commercial Driver's Licenses

A CDL is a specific kind of license that lets drivers operate trucks, cargo vans, buses, and other commercial vehicles. Like regular licenses, they're issued by the Department of Motor Vehicles (DMV). Every driver at your company will need one in order to remain in good legal standing. Any driver without a valid CDL puts your business at risk of being heavily fined or even shut down. Additionally, not getting a CDL means your employee hasn't passed the tests needed to prove they can safely operate the vehicle, which puts them at a higher risk of getting in an accident and hurting themselves or other drivers on the road with them.

First, make sure you're hiring qualified applicants. If you have a local business that doesn't cross state lines, such as a furniture delivery company or a tour bus business, you can hire drivers as young as 18.

However, only people 21 and older can get a CDL that allows them to drive a truck through different states. CDL applicants will also have to submit to a background check, and a high number of at-fault accidents or moving violations may disqualify them.

To pass the written exam and driving test required to get their licenses, employees will need to complete training at a driving school. Some employers offer to pay the fees for these classes for new hires in exchange for these employees agreeing to stay with the company for at least a year, but keep in mind that the classes typically cost upwards of $3,000-$5,000 and they are projected to cost more over time. There's a good chance this may not be an expense you're capable of taking on as a small business. An ideal potential hire will already have a current CDL, but there may be just as many applicants who are looking to start their first trucking job, and need to be guided through the process.

Different trucking businesses may have different licensing requirements. There are three classes of CDL licenses. The three most common classes are Class A, Class B, and Class C. Class A licenses allow drivers to operate nearly all commercial vehicles, including tractor-trailers with a gross combination weight rating of over 26,000 pounds when the towed vehicle is over 10,000 pounds. Class B licenses are a little more restrictive, but drivers can still operate single vehicles without trailers that weigh over 26,000 pounds, or trucks with towed cargo weighing less than 10,000 pounds. These licenses are typically for operating straight trucks and large buses. Class C licenses are the most restrictive, only allowing drivers to operate single vehicles under 26,000 pounds, vehicles towing another vehicle of less than 10,000 pounds, or vehicles with 16 or more riders (Zakhareuski, 2021, para. 3).

Depending on your trucking business, you may also need employees to have a valid endorsement. Different endorsements are needed for jobs that involve driving tank vehicles (N), transporting hazardous materials (H), transporting 16 or more passengers including the driver (P), operating a school bus (S), driving a double or triple trailer (T), and transporting hazardous materials in a tank vehicle (X). Make sure all drivers have the appropriate license and endorsements before getting behind the wheel.

Register With the Department of Transportation and Motor Carrier Authority

Your business also needs certain identification numbers from the United States Department of Transportation (USDOT) and the Federal Motor Carrier Safety Administration (FMCSA) to haul any cargo. The first number you need is the DOT number, which is assigned to all commercial vehicles. It's used to keep an eye on how closely you're following safety regulations and how many violations you have on your record, if any. The motor carrier number, also known as the operating authority, shows what kind of trucking business you run and what sort of cargo you're allowed to transport.

To get both of these numbers, you'll need to fill out a Safety Certification Application and Motor Carrier Identification Report (MCS-150), and submit both forms to the FMCSA. When they receive and review your application, you'll get both numbers, though your operating authority will be in a sort of limbo for the 10 day mandated dispute period. If this period ends without anyone contesting your operating authority, it will be approved.

Unified Carrier Registration

Once you have your USDOT and motor carrier numbers, you can apply for your unified carrier registration (UCR) through the state-level DOT. This registration is not only meant to ensure you have active insurance coverage in your state but in all states where you operate. If you fail to register or your insurance coverage isn't compliant with the program, you may face fines, citations, and other penalties, so it's important to have insurance coverage sorted out before putting anyone on the road. You'll also need to pay an annual fee to the DOT based on how many vehicles are registered to your business.

Keep in mind that if you only operate within one state and never cross state lines, you don't have to register for a UCR, as this only applies to companies dealing with interstate commerce.

International Registration Plan Tag

An international registration plan (IRP) tag is a license plate issued by the DOT in your state. It allows you to operate across state lines, as well as in most Canadian provinces. In addition to registering for the plates, you'll also need to pay an annual renewal fee to remain registered.

Like the UCR, this is only necessary if you plan on delivering cargo in multiple states. Other exceptions include when a vehicle displays restricted plates that limit the area in which they operate, that's if there are separate reciprocity agreements the vehicle operates under, or if the vehicle in question is a school bus, which does not need an IRP tag for field trips and other school events if they fall under the contract with the school district. If these events aren't included in the contract, the bus may instead need a trip permit or apportioned plates, but an IRP isn't necessary.

International Fuel Tax Agreement Decal

The final permit you'll need to get through the DOT is the international fuel tax agreement (IFTA) decal. This decal lets your company have a single fuel decal rather than needing a different one in every state. It's used to simplify how you report fuel usage from your company by rolling all fuel expenses from your company into one report.

The IFTA requires that you file fuel use tax returns on a quarterly basis. You can file these with the state where your company is based, and according to the laws of that state.

BOC-3 Form

If you're running a trucking business that crosses state lines, you'll also need to fill out a BOC-3 form and submit it to the FMCSA to gain your interstate operating authority. This form is meant to ensure that in each state your business operates in, there is someone able to receive any legal complaints and forward them your way. The legal process agents you select for each state must be practicing attorneys in that state. If your company is sued by someone living in a state other than where your central office is located, they can notify you as promptly as possible and the notice will not get lost in the mail.

Standard Carrier Alpha Code

Only certain businesses need to get a standard carrier alpha code (SCAC) before operating. This is necessary if you haul cargo for the military or government, as it gives you clearance to provide these services and makes it easier to identify your company's trucks. You'll also need a SCAC if you're traveling internationally, or if you're hauling an intermodal load. This means you're using two different modes of transportation, such as both a truck and a boat.

Oversize and Overweight Vehicle Permits

Permits for driving oversize and overweight vehicles are issued by state governments, so the rules and regulations differ between states. You'll need to check your local laws to find out which permits you need and where you can get them. Luckily, if you contact the USDOT, they can point you in the right direction and let you know the correct state office you'll need to visit to get these permits, so you don't have to do any guesswork.

Registering Your Business

In addition to making sure you have all the licenses you need to operate, you'll also have to register your company as a business. Through this process, your company becomes a distinct legal entity, which affects paying your employees, filing taxes, and protecting you from being directly harmed by any lawsuits that may be filed against you or your drivers. It also allows you to trademark your name and logo so other companies can't steal it or impersonate you, alongside other legal protections that are offered to different types of registered companies.

Registering your business also allows you to tell the government what kind of ownership you're using. Unregistered businesses are typically considered sole proprietorships by default, but this may not be the case for your business, and you may be missing out on some benefits you would otherwise receive if you filed as an LLC, a partnership, or a corporation.

Sole Proprietorship

In a sole proprietorship, you are the only legal owner of the company. No one else can make official decisions for your company, even if you leave them in charge. This also means you're responsible for all of the financial burdens of the company, including any debts you may incur. In fact, when you're the sole proprietor, your money and your company's money are not legally distinct. This means your personal assets and liabilities can affect your business and vice versa.

Being the sole proprietor of your business is the simplest path, but it's also often considered the riskiest one. Not only will you be the one responsible for all the decision-making for your company, but you'll also be taking on all of your company's debts as your own. If your company is sued for unpaid debt and the judge rules against you, your lender may be able to garnish your income or take other legal action to force you to repay them, such as repossessing loan collateral, rather than being restricted to just the profits of the company. This also means that, since all business debt counts as your own, it can negatively impact your credit score too. If your company goes bankrupt, you'll have to file for bankruptcy yourself.

While there are many downsides to registering as a sole proprietorship, there are some upsides too. For one, you have complete control over your company unless you choose to let someone else take over certain aspects. No one else can submit documents under your name altering big parts of the company, nor can they claim any of the profits for themselves unless you employ them. You'll also keep your start-up costs as low as possible compared to other methods of registering your business. This is the most straightforward method out of all the options available to you. You can certainly change your registration later if you find you prefer one of the other types of businesses, though it's still a good idea to review all your options now and decide what works best for you rather than having to re-register in the future.

LLC

A limited liability company (LLC) means just what the name implies—you limit your liability if something goes wrong with the business. An LLC can have a single owner or multiple owners, so even if you're the only one in charge, you don't have to register as a sole proprietorship by default. Registering your business as an LLC instead will protect you from some of the legal and financial risks that come with running a company. Rather than having your assets and the assets of the business lumped together in the eyes of the law, the company's assets are legally distinct from your own. This means if your company falls into debt and the lenders sue, they can only take money from the company's profits, not your personal savings, property, or other invest- ments. Additionally, if there are multiple company owners and one of your co-owners gets in legal trouble for wrongdoing or negligence, you aren't liable if you aren't found to be at fault.

LLCs can also demonstrate their usefulness when tax season comes around if you have multiple company owners. You'll set up a sepa- rate bank account for the business before you start operating. In most cases, you will pay your own self-employment taxes from the com- pany's profits and losses as well as your own by submitting quarterly payments and filing your tax return in April. However, since there are multiple owners, these profits will be split between each of you. You'll only need to pay taxes on your share of the income. This is different from a sole proprietorship, where profits only go to you and you have to pay taxes on all of the business' income.

Partnership

You can register your business as a partnership if there are two or more co-owners, including yourself. You'll need to fill out a Partnership Agreement form, which serves as a contract between co-owners specifying responsibilities as well as how profits and losses are distributed. You will also have to decide how the burden is divided if the company fails, though you can update this information later if needed.

In addition to a general partnership, there are also limited partnerships (LPs) and limited liability partnerships (LLPs). In an LP, there are both general partners, who own the business and deal with its operations, and limited partners, who merely invest. Limited partners have less liability, but also a smaller share of the profits and less say in how the company operates. General partners all share liability for the business. If you want to protect yourself from negligence and malpractice claims against other general partners, you can register as an LLP instead, where all partners are liable only for their own actions.

Corporation

If you're running a large operation with many employees all fulfilling different roles, registering as a corporation may be the best fit for you. There are C-Corporations (C-Corps) and S-Corporations (S-Corps). In a C-Corp, the business is treated as a completely separate legal entity from its owners, and it can be sued and have its profits taxed on its own. This business structure gives you the greatest personal asset protection. Rather than having one or two owners, C-Corps generally have a board of directors who make decisions about the company together, and owners become shareholders.

S-Corps are similar to C-Corps, but instead of the business' profits being taxed separately, income and losses are passed on to individual shareholders' taxes. This means you get to avoid getting taxed twice on profits, paying for both the business' taxes and your own income taxes, but there are also certain limitations like the company only offering one type of stock and only allowing for a maximum of 100 shareholders.

When you first create your business, you probably won't have to look after so many people, so registering as a corporation is usually unnecessary. This is a more viable option for businesses that have multiple branches across the nation or international companies. However, you may need to change your business registration to a corporation later on if your company grows large enough.

Choosing a Type of Business

To register your business, you must decide which of these formats works best for your goals and the goals of any co-owners who might be running the company with you. Consider the unique needs of your business before making this decision, as well as how trustworthy your business partners are. Speak with your co-owners if you have them and discuss any concerns or opinions they have, as this should be a choice that you are all comfortable with. When in doubt, speak to an expert who can recommend the best way to register your business in order to protect your assets and lower your tax burden.

For most new trucking companies, an LLC is the best fit. This is because it provides the most ideal balance between flexibility and protection for a small-sized business. You have personal protection against lawsuits and any losses the business incurs, and you aren't legally responsible for any illegal actions your co-workers may take. At the same time, you have much more flexibility than you would have if you registered as a corporation, as corporations need to follow a more rigid set of rules for their operations in order to avoid legal trouble. This makes LLCs an ideal option for the majority of businesses of this scale, but again, consult an expert if your company has unique needs or if you want to explore all of your avenues.

Registering Your Name and Home Base

For all business models, you'll need to register your company name and the location that serves as your central operating hub. The name you use for your company doesn't have to be the same as the one you use on legal documents. You can use a "doing business as" name for your operating name, such as "Joe's Trucking" or "Johnson's Shipping." This serves as a fictitious, front-facing name that protects your privacy and the privacy of the consumers paying your company. In some states, a "doing business as" name is required, while in others you only need them if your business name is different from your legal name. Check your state's laws on the topic, which will also include information about how to register the fictitious name.

Next, select a location for your base of operations. You'll need this location to file taxes and to create a bank account for your business. It will also be the location where any important documents from government agencies are delivered, so don't just put down a location you have no plans of visiting every day. You personally don't have to be there all the time, but there should be someone there who can forward these important documents to you.

Remember that you'll have to register your company in each state where you conduct business, so, if your trucks cross state lines, make sure you look into the requirements for each state you pass through. In your home state, register as a domestic entity. In all other states where you do business, register as a foreign entity. You'll need to do this if you have an LLC, partnership, corporation, or nonprofit corporation, but you likely won't have to complete this step if you're operating a sole proprietor business. In most states, you'll need to register with either the Secretary of State's office, a Business Bureau, or a Business Agency.

How to Set Up an LLC

The idea of registering your business as an LLC might sound a little intimidating at first, but like many other parts of establishing your business, it's mainly just a matter of knowing what forms to file and when to file them. You'll have to follow both federal and state guidelines, so read up on these before you begin the registration process so you don't experience any unforeseen delays. If you follow the right steps, this should be a fairly painless process.

Filing the Right Forms

Registration begins with obtaining an LLC Articles of Organization Form. You can get these forms from your state's Secretary of State website and print them out, or visit the office in person. Fill this form out with all relevant information, including the name you've chosen for your company. This name needs to be unique within your state, so read through the publicly available list of current LLCs to avoid choosing a duplicate. Your name also cannot include words that suggest your business is registered as a different type of company, such as 'incorporated,' 'insurance,' or 'corporation,' or that indicate the business is owned by the city. Additionally, you must end your company name with either "Limited Liability Company" or LLC.

Once you have your name, continue filling out the other information requested on the form. These forms usually ask for the location of the central office, the business purpose, the names of all initial members, and any registered agents who can receive legal documents for you. Then submit the form to the Secretary of State office, along with the filing fee and any annual fees your state may have. Don't forget to include an LLC Operating Agreement if you have co-owners, and you want to clearly define the liabilities, responsibilities, and profit distributions for all parties.

Other State-Based Requirements

Some states have unique requirements for registering your business as an LLC, so it's important that you look into what the policies are for the states your business will operate in. For example, some states require that you publish a Notice of LLC Formation in one or more newspapers for a certain amount of time before being able to register. This must be done prior to submitting the Articles of Organization form. States may also have their own specific rules for naming your business, such as profanity guidelines and references to trademarked properties. If you want to avoid your application getting denied and having to file your registration forms multiple times, make sure your business is in compliance with all state regulations.

Registering for Taxes

In addition to registering as a business, you'll also need to register with the Internal Revenue Service (IRS) so your business has an identification number that can be submitted on tax forms. This number is known as an employer identification number (EIN). Both you and any employees will use this number when filing your taxes, and it will also be printed on any W-2 forms or other forms that record employee payments. As a trucking company, you'll likely employ many drivers, but you need an EIN even if you don't hire employees because you'll still have to do your taxes.

The IRS also requires you to sign up with the Electronic Filing and Tax Payment System (EFTPS), which allows you to make payroll tax payments. These taxes include Social Security and Medicare taxes as well as the federal unemployment tax.

Local Permits and Compliance With Local Ordinances

Registering your business on the federal level should be your first step, but not your last. You must also make sure you're completely registered on the state level as well in order to comply with all local laws that affect your business. This means paying state payroll taxes through local revenue offices, as well as researching and following any laws that specifically apply to small businesses within your state and the states you're operating in.

State Taxes

Your EIN is all you need for federal taxes, but you'll need to register for state taxes too. You can do so through your state's taxing authority or revenue department. Since "doing business in a state triggers state income tax, sales tax, excise taxes, and state employment taxes," (Murray, 2019, para. 13) you may also need to sign up for your state's payroll tax payment system too. This process is a little different in every state so check with the relevant state taxing authority for more information and guidance.

Following State and Local Regulations

Specific regulations for your business vary across state lines. However, there are some common ones that apply nearly everywhere. For example, you'll have to follow local zoning laws, which dictate where you can and cannot run your business from. You may not be able to put your office in a primarily residential area, or too close to geographic features like lakes and marshlands. You will also need to submit to a fire inspection on an annual basis in most states. This ensures you're compliant with the fire code and minimizes your risk of property damage and injury to yourself and your employees by reducing the risk of a fire occurring on the property, so it's in your best interest to get regular inspections.

For any other regulations that may impact your business, such as labor laws, advertisement restrictions, antitrust laws, and regulations for minimizing your environmental impact, see the relevant local offices for more detailed information.

Checklist and CDL Minded Approach

There are many important considerations to make when you're finding your footing as a new company. As you proceed through the registration process and acquire all relevant licenses and permits, ask yourself the following questions:

1. **What type of business structure is the right fit for your trucking business?** Consider whether you want to be the sole owner of your company or if you will have co-owners, the size of the business, and whether you want greater flexibility or protection from liability and debt.

2. **Will you be an owner-operator, or will you hire a driver?** If you plan to employ drivers, you'll need to register to pay taxes on payroll, but you can expand your business' reach much further and make more profits.

Answering these questions will help guide you through the licensing process so you can get on the road even sooner.

Fill out this checklist as you get your licenses and registrations so you can keep track of what you've already done and what you still have to do.

License, registration, or permit	Applicable to your business?	Complete?
CDL		
Federal DOT and Motor Carrier Authority Numbers		
Unified Carrier Registration		
IRP tag		
IFTA decal		
BOC-3 form		
SCAC		
Oversize/overweight vehicle permits		
Articles of Organization form		
Local newspaper article		
EIN registration		
State taxes registration		
Local permits		

CHAPTER 2

Accounting and Bookkeeping Basics

Many first-time business owners make the mistake of assuming the accountant they hire will take care of all the financials for them, so they don't bother to learn about what goes on with their money. This means if there's ever an issue, you're completely out of the loop, even though you may be legally liable for company debts or instances of fraud. You don't want to be caught off-guard, and as the owner of your company, you should have a basic understanding of all accounting principles relevant to running your business. This way, if there's ever any trouble or if you need to make a business decision that could affect your finances, you'll know enough to help manage the problem or avoid an issue entirely.

While good financial literacy is a key skill for you to have when starting your own business, you may not know much about it when you're just starting out. In this chapter, we'll look at some basic accounting terms and principles and how they apply to the way you run your business. We'll also look at the bookkeeping process and the different statements and balance sheets that should be kept as part of your company's records. This knowledge is by no means an in-depth, exhaustive look at nitty-gritty financial details, but it will keep you from making the biggest mistakes that cost many small business owners lots of money and harm their businesses. Whether you decide to hire an accountant for your company or not, knowing basic financial principles and using them to guide your decisions will improve your company's chances of initial and long-term success.

Controlling costs is one of the most important considerations when expanding or altering the way your business operates. Though there are many new trucking companies launched each year, "only 15% of newly formed trucking companies make it to their second year of operation, some of it due to truckers being unaware of how to control costs" (Marcom, 2017, para. 1). If you try to expand too quickly and your spending gets out of control, you may become one of the many businesses that are gone almost as soon as it opens. Learning financial basics will help you avoid this fate, showing you how to anticipate and adjust for new expenses, as well as tracking how much money is being made and spent by your company. With this knowledge, you'll have a much easier time ensuring your company turns a profit and stays in business.

Accounting Terms to Know

There are some basic accounting terms that everyone involved in making financial decisions for a business should know. These include more straightforward terms like profits and expenses, then slightly more complicated ideas like equity and depreciation. Keep in mind that some of these terms are frequently misused outside of the financial industry, so you may find that a term you thought you knew is a little different from how you previously understood it. Knowing all of these terms' correct definitions will help you get a better idea of your company's financial needs and how to manage them.

Revenue

Your revenue is your gross income, meaning it's all the money you make through regular business operations before taxes and other costs eat into it. It includes all sales and any checks you cash from your customers, though it does not include money you gain from non-business sources such as loans.

Expenses

Your expenses are all the costs associated with running your trucking business. These expenses occur regularly, and they may be one-time purchases that support the business' continued ability to operate or regular, recurring costs. They include costs like payroll, truck financing, rent for the company office, insurance, and fuel. Some expenses will be the same between different months like building rent, while others such as fuel and payroll may vary depending on how much work you're doing that month.

Profit/Net Income

Your profit, also referred to as your net income, is how much of the money you make that would remain after paying all your expenses. To calculate it, subtract your expenses from your revenue. If your profit is positive, your business is making money with its current operating strategy. If it is negative, your expenses outweigh the amount you're making and you're continually losing money. This problem will only get worse if you ignore it, so try to make changes to either increase your revenue or decrease your expenses so you're generating positive profits again.

Gains

A gain is any one-time increase in your business' revenue that doesn't come from your regular operations. Gains give a temporary boost to your cash flow, but you can't rely on them to hold up your business, so you should focus on increasing your revenue. Common sources of gains include the profits from selling real estate and equipment, both of which usually happen when you're downsizing. This means having gains isn't necessarily a good thing in all contexts, even if you're making money. It could indicate you no longer have enough revenue to keep these assets.

Losses

Losses are the opposite of gains. These are one-time transactions too, but instead of making money, they're instances when you lose money on the sale of an asset. While losses have a negative impact on your financial situation, they aren't always necessarily bad. For example, selling an old vehicle to purchase a new one counts as a loss because you paid more for the vehicle when you bought it than you're getting from selling it, but old trucks need to be replaced eventually to avoid potential accidents or breaking down on the side of the road. Still, you should keep a close eye on your losses and ensure you can afford them before making any big moves.

Assets

An asset is anything owned by your company that has value, and that can be converted into cash. Assets may be liquid, which includes both money in the company's bank account and any property that can easily and readily be sold for money, or illiquid, which means they're typically held for a long time and cannot be converted to cash quite so instantly. Your company can have current, liquid assets such as available cash, inventory, and accounts receivable, as well as fixed, illiquid assets like equipment and real estate.

Liabilities

Liabilities include all obligations and debts that apply to your business. Debts in this case usually refer to money owed on loans, which you must pay back gradually over time from your revenue, as well as any interest charged on those debts. As for obligations, this includes expenses such as employee wages, taxes, and accounts payable.

Equity

In some cases, equity refers to your share of ownership in your company. If you're the sole proprietor, you have 100% of the company's equity, while if you have co-owners your equity is divided between all of you, sometimes unevenly. However, in finance, equity can also mean the difference between your assets and your liabilities. If your assets are worth more than your liabilities, your equity will be positive. In other words, if the current market value of a truck is $80,000 and your remaining auto loan balance is $60,000, you have $20,000 of positive equity.

Equity can also be negative, which occurs when your liabilities outweigh the value of your assets. Let's say you bought a truck with a $100,000 loan. After using the truck for a few years, wear and tear have decreased its value to $60,000, but you weren't able to keep up with loan payments and you still owe $80,000. In this case, you would have $20,000 of negative equity. Even if you sold the truck and put all of that money toward the loan, you would still owe that $20,000. Ideally, then, you want to keep your equity positive whenever possible, but sometimes the decreasing value of the equipment is inevitable when you're using it every day.

Accounts Payable

Accounts payable includes all the money your business owes in exchange for goods and services. These account for your short-term debts, and they make up part of your total liabilities.

Accounts Receivable

Accounts receivable is any money owed to your business for the work you've provided to your customers. If you accepted a job and haven't gotten paid for it yet, it's part of your accounts receivable as an invoice balance. It only remains there until it is paid by the customer. This is one of the most important things to organize well, as losing track of a debt a customer owes you might mean you never get paid for that job at all.

Credit and Debit

Credit and debit are two different forms of payment. A credit entry decreases the value of an asset account while increasing your liability or equity account. Meanwhile, a debit entry increases an asset or expense account but decreases your liability or equity account. In other words, just like with credit and debit cards, any credits mean you pay a debt off later, while any debits mean you pay the debt off right away.

Depreciation

While some assets can appreciate in value the longer you hold onto them, meaning their market price increases, others experience depreciation, where their value decreases. Depreciation accounts for how much of an asset is used up, or how much of its value it has lost, over time. If an asset like a vehicle loses its value as it gains wear and tear from years on the road, meaning people aren't willing to pay as much for it as they would have when it was new, it undergoes depreciation. In many cases, you can deduct an asset's depreciation from your taxes.

Overhead

Overhead is typically used to refer to the costs of starting your business. More specifically, it means any business costs that aren't directly related to providing a service for your customers. These are operational costs that you have to pay whether you perform any work or not in order to keep your company in business. When you're tracking the spending habits of your company and creating a budget, don't forget that ongoing expenses count as overhead too.

Break-even

Your break-even point refers to how many jobs you would have to do or how much work you would have to take on to make your income equal to your expenses. Your sales should, at minimum, cover your total costs. It's better for your sales to be well over your expenses so you are generating a profit, of course, but when your business is just starting out it may take some time to reach this point.

Calculating your break-even point gives you important insight into what your sales goals for your business should be if you want to remain operational. It can indicate that your costs are too high or the prices you charge are too low if you're not making enough money on the jobs you currently have to break even. Knowing your break-even point will also better equip you to analyze whether or not a new project or expansion would be a good fit for your business.

Financial Statements You Need to Know

Now that you know some basic accounting terms, you'll have an easier time understanding the different financial statements that you should make for your company. These statements help you track your expenses and your income. They also give you a clear frame of reference for evaluating various business decisions so you can see whether or not your business's current financial situation can support these moves.

Profit and Loss Statement

A profit and loss (P&L) statement is one of the best ways to calculate the net income for your trucking business. It's a simple method for comparing your revenue and your costs to determine your profits. Most businesses make a P&L statement on at least an annual basis, but it's typically a good idea to do them quarterly, every three months when you're first starting out and your profits will likely vary a great deal. You can then compile these into one big P&L statement for the year that shows you your average quarterly profits and indicates how healthy your business is.

P&L statements help you familiarize yourself with just how expensive running a business can be. If you're not fully aware of how much you're spending each month, these costs will continue to add up without intervention from you. Once you understand just how much you're spending each month compared to how much you're bringing in, you'll have an easier time making adjustments to lower your biggest expenses.

Since you're only comparing two variables, there are very few components of a standard P&L statement. First, always write down the period of time you're looking at on the statement with specific start and end dates. Then calculate your total gross income, or revenue, for the year or quarter depending on the time period you're analyzing. Make sure to save things like invoice receipts and the balance of checks cashed so you know exactly how much you earned. Next, write down each business expense you incurred during this time. You can split these up into different categories like payroll, fuel, and maintenance so it's easier to see where these costs are coming from. All that's left for you to do is to take your total income and subtract your total expenses, which will give you your profits for the year or quarter.

Use this example and template to calculate your profits and losses.

PROFIT AND LOSS STATEMENT

COMPANY:

FOR THE PERIOD OF:

INCOME	EXPENSES

GROSS INCOME: TOTAL EXPENSES:

PROFITS (INCOME - EXPENSES):

PROFIT AND LOSS STATEMENT

COMPANY: SAMPLE COMPANY, LLC

FOR THE PERIOD OF: JAN 1, 2021 - MARCH 31, 2021

INCOME	EXPENSES
CUSTOMER PAYMENTS: $80,000	MAINTENANCE: $10,000
OTHER INCOME: $15,000	FUEL: $5,000
	PAYROLL: $25,000
	LOAN PAYMENTS: $3,000
GROSS INCOME: $95,000	TOTAL EXPENSES: $43,000

PROFITS (INCOME - EXPENSES): $52,000

Cash Flow Statement

In order to run a successful business, you need a steady, reliable cash flow. If you don't know how much money is coming in each month, or if this amount varies significantly, you won't be able to plan for the future. A cash flow statement helps you monitor this factor by detailing the amount of actual cash your company has on hand, this does not include total assets. It also helps you make fairly accurate predictions about your future cash flow, which enables you to make smart decisions with your future finances in mind. You also get a better picture of how cash is being used or generated in your operations, as well as in financing and investing.

Your cash flow is a little different from your profits. It only accounts for money coming in, not necessarily the value of other assets, and it's calculated differently than in the P&L statement. You may have non-cash revenue that boosts your profits but that doesn't actually increase your cash flow, which can be a problem if you have very high expenses you need to pay off right away. Because of this, it's possible for a company to have positive profits but still go out of business because the cash flow was negative for too long, even if this negative flow would have only been temporary.

To create a cash flow statement, you need to know your operating, financing, and investing cash flows. Operating cash flow shows how much money you generate from regular operations. Take the money you make from sales and subtract operating expenses, including income tax payments, payroll costs, interest payments, purchases of operational goods and services, and rent payments on your company's office. Financing cash flow includes any cash flow related to how you finance the company itself. Loans you get from banks or investors are positive financing cash flow, while any payments you make on loans or distributions are negative cash flow. Finally, calculate the investing cash flow, which includes any money you spend buying assets or equipment as investments in your business versus any money you gain from selling these assets. Add up the numbers in each of these three categories and you'll have your total net cash flow.

Here's a basic template you can use, as well as an example.

CASH FLOW STATEMENT

COMPANY:

FOR THE PERIOD OF:

OPERATING CASH FLOW:

FINANCING CASH FLOW:

INVESTING CASH FLOW:

NET CASH FLOW
(OPERATING + FINANCING + INVESTING):

CASH FLOW STATEMENT

COMPANY: SAMPLE COMPANY, LLC

FOR THE PERIOD OF: JAN 1, 2021 - MARCH 31, 2021

OPERATING CASH FLOW: $62,000

FINANCING CASH FLOW: $20,000

INVESTING CASH FLOW: ($32,000)

NET CASH FLOW
(OPERATING + FINANCING + INVESTING): $50,000

Balance Sheet

A balance sheet reflects the liabilities, assets, and equity of your company at a given time. It's a good indicator of your overall financial situation, as it can show you when you have far too much debt in comparison to your assets and equity.

To make a balance sheet, start by adding up the value of all your assets. This includes your on-hand cash, money in the company's bank account, the value of equipment and real estate, any inventory, prepaid expenses, and accounts receivable. Then, add up all of your liabilities, such as your loan debts and accounts payable. Finally, determine how much stockholder equity you have and add this to your liabilities. As the name implies, your assets should balance out with your liabilities and equity. This makes sense because you've paid for all the assets you own through either borrowing money, liabilities, or receiving money from investors, which makes up the shareholders' equity. With this information, you can calculate your ratio of debt to equity so you can keep debts under control.

Here's a template and an example balance sheet.

BALANCE SHEET

COMPANY: _____

FOR THE PERIOD OF: _____

ASSETS	LIABILITIES
_____	_____
_____	_____
_____	_____
_____	**EQUITY**
_____	_____
_____	_____
TOTAL ASSETS = _____	LIABILITIES + EQUITY = _____

BALANCE SHEET

COMPANY: SAMPLE COMPANY, LLC

FOR THE PERIOD OF: JAN 1, 2021 - MARCH 31, 2021

ASSETS	LIABILITIES
CASH: $40,000	LOAN DEBTS: $140,000
EQUIPMENT: $150,000	ACCOUNTS PAYABLE: $8,000
PREPAID EXPENSES: $4,000	
ACCOUNTS RECEIVABLE: $10,000	
	EQUITY
	STOCKHOLDER EQUITY: $56,000
TOTAL ASSETS = $204,000	LIABILITIES + EQUITY = $204,000

Accounting Systems

Different businesses use different accounting systems to keep their financials in order. While the numbers themselves don't change, the way you keep track of them matters. There are two main systems that you can use. You can either account for your revenue and expenses as soon as they're incurred, known as an accrual-based system, or account for them when you receive or pay money, known as a cash-based system. Decide which system you will use first so you'll always be consistent, as trying to mix them up can lead to confusion and missed or doubled payments. Once you choose the right system for you, keep your books daily, so you never forget and you always have a good idea of your current financial situation.

Accrual-Based System

In an accrual-based system, you count income and expenses as soon as the transaction occurs. The money may actually be paid or received a few days later or even further into the future, but you record these changes in your finances as soon as you know they're coming. For example, let's say you complete a job and the customer has 30 days to pay you. In an accrual-based accounting system, you would record the payment as income as soon as you completed the job and sent out the invoice, regardless of when the customer actually pays you. The same is true for any expenses—record expenses as you buy things, not when you actually post a payment for them.

An accrual-based system is more accurate, as you get a better picture of the income and expenses that affect your business within a single month. Otherwise, you might have a lot of expenses for fuel costs from a job in one month and not get the payment for the job until the next, which could leave you with a negative cash flow even if the payment is actually much more than the expenses. However, this method can be a little more complicated because you're accounting for money you don't have or haven't yet spent, which means it might not line up with your bank account.

Cash-Based System

A cash-based system is an easier alternative to an accrual-based system. A cash-based system is a good option if you want to keep your finances as simple and straightforward as possible. It's often a more ideal method for many small businesses, and it can be a good fit for your trucking business if you don't want to get too bogged down in making financial calculations and tracking payments that haven't happened yet

In a cash-based system, you only count income when you actually receive the money, and you only count expenses when the money actually leaves your account. You don't recognize these transactions until cash leaves or enters your hands. This gives you an accurate picture of what you have available to you at any time. Note that you may have months where your income is much higher than your expenses or vice versa, which seems less ideal at first. However, your actual net profits will not change, and these numbers won't seem so unusual when you look at quarterly or annual reports. It's worth considering using a cash-based system if you want to make your finances as intuitive as possible.

Accounting & Bookkeeping Mistakes Most People Make and How to Avoid Them

Accounting mistakes that seem small at first can result in big issues if they aren't corrected quickly. When you're dealing with finances, every penny matters, and getting tripped up by small mistakes can be a problem for a company of any size. Some common mistakes to avoid include failing to stick to your plans, not budgeting, making data entry errors, not backing up your files, trying to take on too much of the financial management yourself, and improperly categorizing income and expenses.

Not Following Accounting Procedures

If you spend the necessary time to understand what good accounting procedures look like, which you already have by reading this far into the book, you owe it to yourself to follow through on what you've learned. Turn accounting into a regular system so everyone you employ knows how to play their part. Take all the time you need to gather all necessary information from vendors to make your financial statements. Create a standardized checklist so you always remember to keep track of this information. Write your accounting policy down so everyone can follow it without having to come to you with their questions. When you commit to following a smooth accounting protocol, keeping track of your finances will become second nature.

Working Without a Budget

A budget gives you a good idea of how much you can afford to spend before it becomes a problem for your company. If you don't have one, there's a good chance you're going to get carried away and spend far too much money without any way to cover these expenses. Before long, you'll end up with tons of debt, which can be difficult if not impossible to pay off if you don't have enough revenue sources to keep up with it, especially since you're paying interest on what you owe.

Additionally, having a budget can help you create and write down your realistic financial goals. You'll have a good idea of how much you're making versus the weight of your total expenses, so you'll know how profitable your business is and how much you can expect it to grow. Once you have a good picture of what realistic expectations for your company would be, always write these objectives down so you can make sure that every decision you make brings you closer to achieving your goals.

Making Data Entry Errors

When you're dealing with a high volume of incoming and outgoing transactions, mistakes happen. Something as small as writing down an extra zero or accidentally changing a three to a five can seriously throw off your finances, as you might believe you have more or less money than you actually do. Accuracy is important, so make sure you're always double-checking your numbers and scanning for mistakes. Scan for unusual transactions, and if you notice any, review your records to see if there could be a mistake.

Additionally, help prevent data entry errors by checking the accuracy of all balances on a monthly basis. Create a system where you set aside some time each month to perform a bank reconciliation, double-checking that all bank records match up with actual purchases and payments. Perform accounts receivable and payable reconciliations as well.

Not Having Backups

If you only have a single copy of an important document like payment records or financial statements, losing that copy is a big problem. Always keep backups so you have access to files in case paper copies go missing or a computer breaks and you lose your digital files. Double-check that all backups are accurate and up-to-date. You can even try to use the backup files exclusively and see if you can still run your business as usual, which confirms that you have complete copies of everything you need to function.

Taking on Too Much Responsibility

While some company owners make the mistake of completely ignoring finances, others make the mistake of getting too involved in the day-to-day accounting needs of their business. As an owner, you have a lot of jobs to do, and your time is probably better spent somewhere other than writing down a list of all the checks you deposited that day and cross-referencing them with your bank account. For these routine tasks, it's usually a good idea to hire a dedicated accountant who can manage them for you and offer financial advice so you can focus on making big picture decisions with this information. You can also outsource tax planning and preparation. This not only saves you time but also means a qualified accountant will show you how to lower your tax liability while still being compliant with all tax laws, saving you money.

Incorrectly Categorizing Expenses and Income

Any money that comes into your business or goes out must be categorized appropriately. Otherwise, you might be overreporting your income or incorrectly separating deductible expenses from non-deductible ones. This can artificially increase how much you owe in taxes. If you assume you have more money than you really do, you might spend more, only to find out you can't cover it. If an expense slips through the cracks, you might not realize until it's past the payment due date, so you will owe interest and late fees. All of these outcomes can disrupt your business, which is why it's so important to be accurate when cataloging your income and expenses.

Checklist and CDL Minded Approach

If you're still not entirely certain what your financial statements should look like, try searching for examples from other companies. You can practice your financial analyst skills, using their reports to consider which areas are the biggest problems and what you would do to fix them if you owned that business. With this practice, you'll then be ready to make the right decisions for your own company when the time comes.

Now, apply what you've learned in this chapter about accounting so you can create your own financial statements for your business. You can start with your own personal finances to get the hang of things, then make a smooth transition to creating financial statements for your business.

Follow this checklist to ensure your company finances are in order:

Task	Tips	Complete?
Write out and categorize all sources of income	Use categories like job invoices, asset sales, and interest on bank accounts	
Write out and categorize all expenses	Split into categories such as fuel costs, maintenance, rent, and insurance	
Create a profit and loss statement	Use this statement to determine the profitability of your current business model	
Create a cash flow statement	See where your biggest cash sinks are so you can fix them	
Create a balance sheet	Keep balance sheets and compare them to future months	
Choose an accounting system	Accrual-based can work for some businesses, but cash-based is more straightforward	
Create a system for monthly financial reviews	Set a date at the start or end of each month and stick to it	

CHAPTER 3

The Clutter Proof System— Setting Up Your Finances

C lutter is a nightmare for any business trying to keep track of its finances. In accounting, the more complex your business is, the more important it is to reduce clutter as much as possible. In a trucking business, where you might be arranging deliveries for multiple different jobs with many different drivers across plenty of different states, all at the same time, it's very easy for important payment records, invoices, and receipts to get lost in the clutter. This can lead to unpaid bills, incorrectly reporting information on your taxes, and, occasionally, legal trouble. In some cases, miscalculating your finances because you're missing information, or you don't have a good system in place for tracking and categorizing everything, means you're more likely to overspend, which could put the longevity of your CDL business in danger.

You don't have to go completely minimalist, but a little organization goes a long way toward making accounting as easy and stress-free as possible. This is where the Clutter Proof System comes in.

What Is the Clutter Proof System?

If you want to really embrace CDL-minded accounting strategies, you need to use the Clutter Proof System (CPS). With the CPS, you can quickly and easily reorganize your physical and digital storage systems to make retrieving stored information as easy as possible. It's a way to revolutionize accounting procedures and get all your affairs in order, totally stress-free, and without the need for any prior accounting experience. It's similar to another CPS, Child Protective Services: if you don't use a clutter-proof system for your finances, you aren't taking proper care of your business, which is your brainchild. You don't want to risk having your business "taken away" if it goes bankrupt. By reducing clutter and getting your affairs in order, you'll spend less time looking for misplaced documents and more time focusing on financial analysis and running your business. Make no mistake about it, maintaining organization is one of the most crucial things you can do for yourself and your company.

The Importance of Staying Organized

If you struggle to stay organized, you've almost certainly had moments where you misplaced an important document or another item, and you spent more time looking for it in a panic than you would have liked. The thought of losing something you need is equal parts frustrating and terrifying, but it's also entirely avoidable. All you have to do is stick to a clearly laid out organizational system so you know exactly where things are at all times. It's much easier to find the paperwork you're looking for if it's inside a neat, labeled folder in a filing cabinet than it would be if the paperwork was buried in your desk drawer and mixed together with other documents. Give yourself the advantage of routine organization and you'll avoid many of the annoyances that would otherwise plague you.

Staying organized offers plenty of benefits. For one, if you can easily look back at your expenses and identify which ones are tax-deductible, you'll be able to include them all on your tax returns, reducing your tax obligation. This can save your business a lot of money if you're taking advantage of all possible deductions. You'll also be able to prepare your accounts much faster at the end of the fiscal year since you can quickly retrieve the information you need rather than having to look back at dozens of individual checks and receipts scattered across many different locations without rhyme or reason. If you take stock of your income and expenses as you go, and keep this information handy, this will help you plan out your quarterly tax payments as well, and you'll know exactly how much you either owe or will be getting back on your tax return. You'll also know if the sales and use tax are applicable to your business and if you're liable for paying it to your state's Division of Taxation. The easier it is to get accurate information, the less risk there is of over-or underpaying your taxes, which would mean your business would no longer be in compliance with tax codes. Simple organization strategies can help you avoid any fines or legal troubles.

Organization also helps you make important decisions about how you should run your business and which decisions will bring you closer to your goals without also bringing you closer to the risk of bank-ruptcy. When you know your current expenses and how they stack up against your revenue, you can decide if you can afford to take on expenses associated with expansion, or if you need to focus on increas-ing your business' income first. The organization of your business is as strong as your weakest link, so you must correct any issues as soon as possible. You can then use this information to make the appropriate changes and improvements to how you run your business, whether these improvements are on the customer end to attract more business or they have to do with internal operations.

When you understand your current financial situation, you'll also have a much easier time fulfilling payment obligations. You'll know how much you can afford to pay on loans without overexerting your income, and you'll also have an easier time planning your spending so you can always afford to pay your employees. Additionally, when you have all your information at your fingertips, you won't have to go looking for it if you apply for a new loan so you can supply this infor-mation to creditors right away. Should you ever decide to sell your business, you'll know how much it makes and what a fair sale price would be. If your company grows large enough that you have multiple shareholders who receive dividends, or if your business is a partner-ship where you share profits and losses, you'll have an easier time dividing and paying out the necessary cut of the profits to all parties.

In short, organization is a way to fast-track nearly all of your accounting tasks. If you start out on the right foot, it's much easier to get and stay organized than it will be if you wait months or years and then realize you can't operate efficiently without organization. With the CPS, you can break the overall accounting and financial management process down into a series of straightforward, easily manageable tasks. This allows you to make regular updates and to refer back to past records without wasting time. Use the CPS from day one to put your business on the right track to success.

Your Business Bank Account

Whether you choose a company model where your finances are separate from those of your business, like an LLC, or where there is no legal difference, like a sole proprietorship, your business should have its own checking account. This allows you to easily see how your business' profits change over time without having to sort through all the times you used your personal debit card to buy a coffee. Keep all your personal and business expenses separate, as this will make it easier to see how much money you have in the bank at any one time.

To keep things as simple as possible, deposit all checks into this account first. Then pay yourself out of the account's funds. This is a lot easier to keep track of for recordkeeping purposes than if you directly deposited a check into your own account, as you might forget to count that income when calculating your company's revenue. Pay all of your business expenses out of this account as well so you can easily see all of your outgoing payments.

Since you'll want to keep track of your monthly finances, as this will make it easier to complete quarterly and annual financial statements, opt for a bank account that has month-end cutoffs. You can review all the transactions that took place within a single month and quickly coordinate all your records by keeping everything organized on a monthly basis. If your bank sends you statements halfway through the month, you'll have to calculate your monthly totals yourself, which takes more time and effort and increases the risk of making a costly mistake.

It's also helpful to have both a checking and savings account for your business. Your business checking account should be focused on receiving payments, as well as paying any expenses like utilities and rent. Once you've deposited a check into your checking account, you can then transfer it into your savings account if you want to avoid the risk of spending that money. Use your savings account as a way to set aside funds to cover future expenses like tax payments. It can also hold your business' emergency fund, which is invaluable if your company is hit with any surprise expenses.

Use a Separate Credit Card for Business Expenses

In addition to having separate checking and savings accounts for your business, you should also have a separate credit card. While you don't want to be overly reliant on using credit, and you definitely shouldn't make purchases you can't afford to pay back, paying your expenses on credit can help you simplify your recordkeeping strategy even further. Credit cards let you separate your charges into different categories such as gas, maintenance, food, and more. When you're listing out your expenses at the end of the month, you only need to refer to your credit card statement to see where you spent the most money and where you might consider reducing spending if you're not making as much of a profit as you would have liked. As a general rule, never put personal expenses on your company credit card or vice versa. Continue to keep your business' funds separate from your personal funds.

Even though you're using a credit card, you can still avoid paying high-interest rates and racking up a lot of debt by paying off the card balance in full every month. In fact, if you qualify for a card with no annual fee and a good rewards plan, you can actually save money by getting cashback on your purchases. That said, there may be months where you find yourself unable to pay off the full balance due to a surprise expense, so opt for a card with a lower interest rate as a backup. Smart credit use can be a huge benefit for your company, while careless credit use will put your business in jeopardy. Always check to see if you can afford a purchase before making it, even, and especially, if you're putting it on a credit card, and set money aside to pay off these expenses as soon as you buy something.

Creating a Payment System for Customers

Customer payments are the primary source of income for your business. While this seems like a simple transaction, you can receive payment in a number of different ways, which complicates the process a little. Small businesses might accept cash, checks, credit cards, online payments, mobile payments, transfers through apps like Venmo or Zelle, or any combination of these methods. You'll need to decide which ones you're going to accept so you can tell your customers upfront.

Note that different payment systems can help or hinder your business. For example, if your business only accepts cash so you get your money immediately and you can deposit it right away, this may deter customers who would prefer to pay with a card or electronically. On the other hand, if you only accept electronic or card payments because you don't want to physically go to the bank and deposit cash, this can be an inconvenience for other customers who would rather just hand you money.

Some payment methods may involve processing fees as well. Different credit card providers have different fees for credit payments. Even the method by which you accept the card affects how expensive it is for you as a business owner, as "the average costs for credit card processing ranges from 1.5% to 2.9% for swiped cards, and 3.5% for keyed-in transactions," (Hayashi, 2020, para. 7) with keyed-in transactions meaning credit information is entered manually. Most card and electronic payments have a delay of a day or more before the money leaves the customer's account and ends up in your own, which you'll need to plan around to ensure payments clear before you try to spend them. It's important to keep your fees affordable, not to mention easily manageable, but you should also try to accommodate the needs of as many different customers as possible. Try to offer multiple payment options while still choosing methods that don't take too much of your revenue as fees.

Creating a Payroll System for Employees

If you employ drivers or contract with them, you'll need to make regular payments. The more you can automate this process, the better, since paying wages and salaries is a routine exercise. Make sure you use the same method each time, always paying your employees on the same day in the payment period, and paying them for the same period of time. Most companies pay on a weekly or biweekly basis, so try to keep payments consistent, like calculating payroll every other Tuesday and giving employees their wages on Wednesday. You can also choose to pay employees on a per-job basis, but this can turn into a lot of work and too many separate transactions, complicating the process. Stick to a regular schedule to keep things easy on yourself. This also allows employees to plan for when they're going to get their money, which is more convenient for them.

You'll also need to make sure you're withholding the right taxes for different employees. When you hire a worker, make sure they fill out the proper tax forms. In most cases, they'll need to complete a W-4 form. If you use an accounting software designed for small businesses, most come with a payroll feature, which will assist you in this process.

Independent Contractors

Some of the people who work for you may not be employees, but independent contractors instead. You do not need to withhold any income taxes for independent contractors, as they are considered self-employed. However, you still need to keep track of how much you've paid to each independent contractor hired for a job by your business. Most American business owners should report "payments of $600 or more in a calendar year on a Form 1099" (Administration for Children and Families, 2018, para. 7) which are then submitted at the end of the year.

Preparing a Budget

If you've ever tried to create a budget for your personal finances, you know that half the difficulty comes from finding the right numbers to fill it out. You need to have a good idea of your income and expenses in various categories, which means you may have to track your spending for a few months before you're ready to make your budget. Luckily, staying organized will make creating a budget easier, as you can quickly pull relevant income and expense numbers from different documents. Creating a budget makes staying organized easier in return, as you get to lay out your plan for the next month and all that's left is to follow it. You collect all relevant information in the same place, so you don't have to go looking for it each time you're considering making a purchase; you can simply refer to your budget.

Budgeting has plenty of other benefits as well. It will support your efforts to ensure your business is sustainable and that it can thrive no matter what bumps may appear on the road. You can use your budget as a reference point for evaluating how feasible any changes in your business model would be, giving you a good idea of whether or not you could afford to make them. You'll see problem areas where you may need to cut back on spending or find ways to increase your revenue. Also, if you want to apply for loans and other funding, a budget will help you demonstrate to creditors that you're fiscally responsible and increase your chances of approval.

While sticking to your budget can be a little tricky sometimes, actually making it is a fairly straightforward task when you're well organized. To increase your budget, you'll need to determine your income and weigh it against your fixed, variable, and one-off expenses.

Step 1: Add up Your Income

Start by taking stock of all your income sources. If you haven't started operating yet, these will just be estimates, but you'll have more accurate numbers once your business has been up and running for a few months. For now, consider how much you might realistically make from fulfilling customer orders and any other sources of revenue for your type of CDL business, and write the total down on your budget sheet.

Step 2: Calculate Your Fixed Costs

Fixed costs are costs that remain the same each month. These costs aren't affected by how many jobs you complete. Your trucks could remain parked for a whole month and you would still have to accommodate these expenses. For example, the rent you pay for your office building is a fixed cost, since you know how much it will be each month. Other fixed costs that apply to most CDL businesses include permits, insurance, loan payments, and some utilities.

Again, if you don't yet have real data from your business, you can use projected costs to make this calculation. Once you know what your fixed costs are, write these down in the appropriate area on the budget sheet.

Step 3: Estimate Your Variable Expenses

Unlike fixed expenses, variable expenses get their name because they vary from month to month. They are often dependent on how many jobs you take on, but they can come from other sources as well. As an example, fuel costs are variable, since performing many jobs that take your drivers across multiple state lines will cost you more in fuel payments than if you only did a few jobs and didn't have to drive very far to complete them. Other variable expenses come from sources such as tolls, vehicle maintenance, replacement tires, and food and lodging costs for drivers.

At first, you'll need to tally these kinds of expenses on a month-by-month basis. In time, they will start to level out, even though they can still vary. You'll develop a better idea of what your variable expenses will look like in busy months and slow months, which will make your predictions more accurate and improve the effectiveness of your budget. Once you have a good estimate of your variable expenses, write these down as well.

Step 4: Predict One-Off Expenses

Some one-off expenses are surprises, like a replacement for a piece of equipment that suddenly breaks but isn't so expensive you have to take a loan out for it. You can't really budget for these, though if you find you have these kinds of emergency expenses often, you can set aside some emergency money in your budget that goes into your savings if it's not used. However, some one-off expenses are entirely predictable, and planning for them in advance can save you a lot of time and stress.

Think about anything you know you have to buy within the next month. Maybe your work computer is slow and you're going to buy a new one two weeks from now. Maybe you're planning on taking a business course or attending a CDL industry conference with an admission fee. By putting these costs in your budget, you can set aside the money for them ahead of time and make sure you still have enough left over to cover all your other expenses. The fewer surprises you have lurking around the corner, the better for your business, so be sure to note down any upcoming purchases.

Step 5: Put It All Together

Now that you have all your income and expense estimates, it's time to use them to create your budget. Add your fixed, variable, and one-off expenses to get your total expenses. Then subtract this from your income, which will give you your profits. You'll also be able to easily see how your incoming cash flow compares to your outgoing cash flow so you can identify any possible issues before they become mountains of debt.

In a budget, every dollar you have should be accounted for. Ideally, your income should outweigh your expenses. If this is the case for you, then you should decide where you want to put that extra money. Maybe you want to put it into the checking or savings account of your company, or maybe you would prefer to invest it into growth for your company, so it would become an expense. Once you've delegated all of your income to either spending or saving, you can analyze your budget to see if there are any areas where spending is out of control. If your expenses outweigh your income, or if it's a close enough call that one bad month might put you in the red, this indicates you might need to either reduce spending or aim to increase income. Budgeting lets you quickly see problem areas at a glance, which is why they're such a useful tool for any business.

To get you started, here's a sample budget you can use when crafting your own:

BUDGET SHEET

COMPANY:

FOR THE PERIOD OF:

INCOME	FIXED EXPENSES
	VARIABLE EXPENSES
ONE-OFF EXPENSES	

BUDGET SHEET

COMPANY:

FOR THE PERIOD OF:

INCOME	FIXED EXPENSES
FULFILLED ORDERS: $15,000	OFFICE RENT: $1,200
INVESTMENTS: $3,000	INSURANCE: $800
MISC. INCOME: $2,000	LOAN PAYMENTS: $2,000
TOTAL INCOME: $20,000	**VARIABLE EXPENSES**
	FUEL: $2,300
ONE-OFF EXPENSES	FOOD AND LODGING: $1,700
NEW WORK COMPUTER: $1,200	TOLLS: $200
CDL COURSE: $400	MAINTENANCE: $3,800
TRUCK REPAIR: $2,300	SAVINGS: $4,100

TOTAL INCOME [$20,000] - TOTAL EXPENSES [$20,000] = $0

Paying Yourself

Just as you need to pay your employees, you also need to pay yourself. Some company owners choose to pay themselves last by pouring the money back into growing the business instead. While this does give you some extra capital, it's not something you should be doing if you want to keep both company finances and personal finances in good shape. Not having enough money to pay your personal bills can hurt your business as well, especially if it harms your credit so you no longer qualify for loans with good terms. This will also leave you feeling stressed more often, which can drastically get in the way of running your company.

Paying yourself, whether you need the money or not, reinforces the idea that your work is just as worthy of compensation as any other employee's contributions. You want to pay all of your employees, so you should treat yourself with the same regard you would give to anyone else. Pay yourself a fair wage for the work you're doing, even if it feels a little selfish sometimes. If your business continues to grow and it becomes very successful, you'll know that the payments you took for yourself didn't hurt it in the long run. If it struggles and doesn't end up working out for you, then at least you'll have some savings to look forward to while you contemplate your next move.

Paying Bills

The biggest mistake new company owners make with bills is not preparing for them appropriately with budgeting and saving. If you forget about a bill and getting the statement for it catches you off-guard, you might not have the money to pay it by the end of the month. This means late fees and interest, which makes it even harder to pay what you owe. Go too many months in a row without paying off your bills in full, and you'll have a significant amount of debt draining your income.

In many cases, avoiding late fees can be the deciding factor between making a profit and going into the next year with debt dragging you down. Make sure you keep track of the bills you still need to pay so you don't forget about them when the time comes. You can set up monthly reminders for bill due dates to make sure you don't miss anything. Ideally, you should pay off all your purchases in full, but if that's not something you can afford because of a surprise expense, at least commit to making the minimum payments on all your loans and credit card debt. This means you won't be charged a fee, just interest. While interest can be a problem on its own, it's not nearly as bad as having the whole balance owed plus fines. When you're strapped for cash, do what you can to keep your debt under control until you can pay it off completely.

Accountants and Accounting Software

In the previous chapter, you learned that trying to take on the burden of all the accounting needs of your business is often a mistake. It distracts too much from the other jobs you should be doing to manage your company. To assist you with these duties, and to free up your time for more important tasks, you'll want to hire a professional, experienced accountant that you can trust in order to guide you through complex tax laws and keep an eye on your fiscal health. You can also benefit from buying accounting software, which makes it much easier to track your income and expenses. This lets you quickly hone in on any problem areas and reduces the overall amount of time you have to dedicate to analyzing your finances.

Hiring an Accountant

You might assume that since you have a small business, you don't need to outsource your accounting needs. The truth is that the time, stress, and money your accountant will save you is well worth what you pay them. Ideally, you should opt for a certified public accountant (CPA) rather than an unlicensed accountant. CPAs must meet state qualifications including passing the Uniform Certified Public Accountant Examination and continuing their education outside of college so they are up to date with all tax laws (Murray, 2020, para. 5-6). In contrast, accountants who are not CPAs don't have to take a licensing exam. With a CPA, you can be confident that you're hiring someone who is qualified to offer the best financial advice. They'll help you achieve another type of CPA: "Clutter Proof Accounting."

If you're still hesitant to spend the money to hire a CPA, remember that paying for their services now to ensure you remain compliant with tax laws is much better than hiring them later to help you get yourself out of a mess or to accompany you if you are audited by the IRS. As always, an ounce of prevention is worth a pound of cure, and your CPA provides invaluable prevention against making poorly thought out business decisions and getting into hot water with your taxes. That said, if you do run into trouble, CPAs are qualified to represent your business at a tax audit. This is one of the main reasons why you should hire a CPA over an accountant, as accountants usually cannot perform this service. Even if it seems like an unlikely scenario, it's better to err on the side of caution.

In addition to hiring a CPA, you should also outsource your bookkeeping needs to a freelance or part-time bookkeeper. Your bookkeeper can handle the more routine accounting jobs like tracking your revenue, expenses, and profits, leaving your CPA free to focus on more in-depth analysis. Many CPA firms have both bookkeepers and accountants, so you can go to the same firm for both services.

Investing in Accounting Software

If you want to make the process of tracking your finances as pain-free as possible, buying accounting software is the best thing you can do for yourself. You can quickly update your income and expenses at the end of each day, review your company's financial history, and make sure your spending stays in line with your budget, all from a single program. Additionally, you don't have to fill out any forms by hand, and using accounting software ensures that even if your computer crashes, your financial records will be safe since they're stored through the software.

You have plenty of options when choosing an accounting software, and many of these options are available for as cheap as $10 a month. You can go with a general accounting software like Freshbooks, Quickbooks, or Xero, or you can opt for accounting software that is specifically designed for trucking companies such as RigBooks, Trucking Office, ProTransport, TruckBytes, or McLeod Software. Each option has its own pros and cons.

General accounting software is a "one size fits all" method of managing your accounting needs. These programs are typically easy to use since they're designed to function with many different businesses as well as personal finance needs. Processes like bookkeeping, time tracking, invoicing, budgeting, sales tax management, and bank reconciliation are all automated. You can quickly access your financial statements without hassle, and it's easy to collaborate with your CPA and bookkeeper with these services. However, general accounting software lacks any dedicated features designed with CDL businesses in mind. You can find these kinds of features only if you use trucking-specific accounting software.

Trucking management software offers many unique features that you'll find useful as a CDL business owner. This software can assist with dispatching drivers to different jobs, as well as arranging driver settlements and performing other employee and contractor management services. They can help you keep track of your upcoming invoices so you can stay on top of them until they're paid. You can manage income and expense transactions and automatically create reports on your profits and losses. You'll save time on recurring deductions, and you can easily store information about fuel costs. Using this information will make quarterly IFTA tax payments a breeze. You do lose out on some of the simplicity of more general software, and you may have to pay a little more for these programs, but trucking software gives your business a leg up because it is specifically designed for business owners like yourself. Either way, choose the software you are most comfortable with so you can streamline your accounting process.

Checklist and CDL Minded Approach

Organizing your finances makes it much easier to ensure you're sticking to the budget you've created for your company. With the Clutter Proof System, you'll lay the foundation that will help you achieve lasting success in tracking your finances and keeping costs under control.

To start setting up your finances, follow the steps in this checklist:

Task	Where to Find Resources	Complete?
Open a bank account for your business	PNC, Chase, Wells Fargo, NavyFederal	
Open a credit card for your business	American Express, Amex, Chase, Citi	
Create a payroll and payment system	QuickBooks, ADP, Gusto, Paychex	
Choose an accounting software	Freshbooks, TruckBytes, Trucking Office, RigBooks	
Start preparing your business budget	QuickBooks, Xero, FreeAgent, BillQuick	
Find an accountant to assist you with setting up your finances	State find-a-CPA directories	

CHAPTER 4

The Clutter Proof System—Helping You Keep Track of Your Finances

There's little point in creating a budget and a payroll system if you can't stick to them, and this process starts with keeping track of all relevant financial information. You want to make it as easy as possible for you, your CPA, and your bookkeeper to retrieve this information, so organization and reducing clutter is key. Staying organized also ensures you won't lose track of important records. If you're not reporting the right numbers on your financial statements, you'll skew the results, which makes all the work you put into creating a budget worthless. If you lose track of a big expense and you think you have higher profits than you actually do, not only will you have to pay late fees and interest on that huge expense, but you might also make purchases that your income can't actually support because you think you're spending less than you really are.

Keeping good records that provide accurate numbers will improve the reliability and helpfulness of your financial planning efforts. You'll be able to trust that the numbers you're working with to make your budget and cash flow statement are correct because you have the records to back them up. If you ever need to double-check an unusual number, if you have a payment disagreement with a customer, or if you get audited, you have all your records right at your fingertips. Once you have a record-keeping system that becomes part of your company's daily routine, you'll always know where to look if you need to reference different documents.

Record Keeping

You should keep your records in a way that makes it as easy as possible to both file away information in the proper location and also find what you're looking for, even if it's been months or years since you last looked at a certain document. When everything is in its place, you won't have to remember where things are, because you can trust they'll be in the right spot every time.

To this end, the methods you use for the record-keeping should be simple and easily understood by everyone involved. If drivers are receiving payments, they should know where to file the paid invoices, even if they're not directly responsible for managing finances. Similarly, your CPA should know where to look for these invoices if they need to reference them, so they can do their job without constantly asking you where different documents are. Keep things as straightforward as possible so you have as few filing mistakes as possible, and try to make the organization of records an automatic process. Don't wait until the end of the day to organize, as it may not get done on days that you're busy, and before long you'll have created a huge backlog of unfiled documents. Organize as you go throughout the day so it never takes more than a few seconds at a time to put a file in its proper place.

Make sure you're saving all important information you may need to double-check at a later date, as well as anything you might need to keep records of by law. This includes receipts, logbooks, tax return records, and canceled checks. For maximum efficiency, you'll also need to rotate out old information that's no longer applicable to your business. It also helps to have frequent check-ins with your financial analysis team to make sure you're on top of everything that needs to get done, and that you have all the records you need to complete these tasks.

CDL Minded in Your Receipts

Let's say you're an owner-operator or a driver making a delivery for your company. While on the road, you stop for lunch at a fast-food restaurant. Since you only spent a few dollars, you don't pay much attention to what happens to your receipt. It ends up crumpled up and grease-stained, lost somewhere in the clutter in the passenger-side footwell, or maybe you throw it out with the bag from your meal. Either way, you no longer have it, and now you don't have a reliable way of knowing how much you spent that day. However, the cost of the meals you eat while on the road for a job are actually tax-deductible. Sure, a single meal might not take much money off of what you owe for taxes, but think of the total cost of the meals you would eat in an entire year of truck driving. These expenses can add up fast, and you'd probably rather save the money on your taxes than let this deduction go unused. The best way to ensure you have accurate information about work-related expenses when tax time comes is to save all of your receipts, even if they seem insignificant.

It's easy to keep track of receipts if you can bring them back to the office right away, but it's often harder if you'll be unable to file these receipts away for a few hours, or even days, if you still have to drive through multiple different states. There's a lot of risk when receipts get misplaced and lost. To avoid this, keep a dedicated envelope in every driver's truck where they can put their receipts all in the same place. Once they return, these receipts can then be reviewed and categorized in the right place. For e-receipts, create a folder on your computer or in a cloud to hold all of them. You can further divide these folders by quarter, or by the type of expense to keep them even more organized. Keep receipts of all your expenses, whether they're tax-deductible or not. You can then use them to fill out your monthly profit and loss statements and any other statements you may need them for.

In most cases, it's good enough to have a scanned copy of the receipt on file for future use. This is fine if you only need the receipt to see how much something costs so you can report it on a financial form or for your taxes. However, there are some cases where you'll need to hold onto the original receipt. For example, if there's a chance you might return something, you'll need the original receipt to do so. Many big-ticket items come with warranties, so you'll need to keep the receipts for them in case they break within the warranty period so you can be fully reimbursed.

Save Your Log Books

Just like receipts, it's also important to make sure you hold onto your logbooks. A logbook contains information about driving hours and off-duty activities, including time spent sleeping and eating. A logbook contains information about driving hours and off-duty activities, including time spent sleeping and eating. Essentially, it is a complete record of everything you do while you're on the road. Keeping a logbook is mandated by the FMCSA. Since you're going through all the trouble to fill it out, don't let all that hard work go to waste by misplacing it and losing all the information contained inside. Logbooks are the best way to prove your claims that tax-deductible expenses, like meal costs, occurred while on the job, so you should save them just as judiciously as you do your receipts and any payment records.

If you're using an electronic logging device (ELD) instead of a physical logbook, it's more convenient to keep track of your expenses, but you may also encounter technical difficulties that complicate the process. Before entering in any information, make sure your ELD allows you to save and store this data properly, and that you have access to your history. Back up this information routinely on a separate device just in case the ELD is damaged or suddenly stops working, especially if you only use an ELD and you don't use physical logbooks at all.

Record-Keeping on the Road

It's easy to misplace things when you're driving for the majority of the day, often for multiple days in a row, and you don't have the chance to file important documents right away. To avoid losing them before you return to headquarters, create and stick to a simple filing system while in the truck. This starts with keeping an envelope in the glove box or somewhere else easily accessible where you can store receipts, logbooks, and other papers you want to hold on to. Alongside your receipts and logs, you should also keep a personal use notebook, though you can also use a note-taking or journaling app on your smartphone if you regularly back up your phone.

If you can't get a receipt for an expense for any reason, record it in your notebook so you have some record of the transaction. For example, if you have to stop and wash your truck at a coin-operated facility, you won't get a receipt for this, but you'll still want to keep track of how much it cost you. You can also use this system to keep track of your miles if you're using a personal vehicle for reasons related to the operation of your business. Next to each expense, record the amount, date and time, location, and reason for incurring the cost so you have as complete of a record as possible.

If you employ other drivers, make sure they all follow this system as well. Everyone should use the same method of recording transactions to keep things simple.

Save All Your Tax Return Records

When you file your taxes for the year, you can toss all that information, right? Not so fast. The IRS actually recommends that in most cases, you should "keep records for 3 years from the date you filed your original return" (Internal Revenue Service, 2020, para. 4). This is known as the period of limitations, which is the period during which you are allowed to claim an additional refund or credit by adding or changing the information on your previous tax return, as long as you have documentation. For example, if you forgot to deduct a large expense, you can add the deduction to the tax report for the correct year as long as it falls within this period of limitations. During this time, the IRS can also apply additional taxes to a previous return if they believe you should have paid more. Keeping your records is the best method of defense you have for proving your case against these claims and keeping your tax burden as low as possible.

While you should always keep a copy of your tax returns, they're not the only tax-related documents you should hold onto for the full period of limitations. Other important documents include your quarterly estimated tax payments, insurance documentation, monthly profit and loss statements, warranty information, registration information, maintenance records, canceled checks, bank statements, settlement statements, and business credit card statements. Essentially, anything that provides a number you use on your tax returns should be kept for the full three years. You should be able to quickly and easily answer questions about income and expenses during this timeframe, so you have nothing to fear from an audit or allegations of tax compliance errors, and you can resolve these issues right away.

Note that some financial records you use for your taxes, such as income documentation and loan statements, should not be shredded at the end of the three-year period. You will need to hold onto these for longer, usually seven years, in case you ever get audited. The only documents you should get rid of after the three years are up are ones that are used almost exclusively for your tax returns, like those listed above.

Handle Checks With Care

If you don't carefully review checks, you might miss any instances of fraudulent activity. As a business owner, you probably want to think the best of your employees and co-owners. While it doesn't do anyone any good to be constantly suspicious of the people you work with, that doesn't mean you should turn a blind eye to any possible instances of wrongdoing. It's possible someone might take checks linked to the company bank account and use them for unauthorized or fraudulent purposes. Review all canceled checks from your bank to make sure they were all used to pay for actual business expenses. These should only be expenses you have approved. Giving someone unrestrained access to the checks to make whatever purchases they like will more than likely result in overspending. In this scenario, the budget would fail to consider these unplanned, excessive expenses, which could put your company in a lot of debt. Correct the problem with the responsible employee, taking disciplinary action if it was intentional fraud, and speak to your bank about reversing the charge.

One way you can prevent check forgery is by always taking care to sign your name in a clear, legible way. The more care you take writing your signature, the harder it will be for someone to copy it. If you sign all checks with a random squiggle, you won't be able to tell which checks you actually signed and which ones might have been signed by someone else. A legible signature that is clearly in your own handwriting helps you prove your case if you ever need to claim your signature was forged on a check or another important document.

Out With the Old, in With the New

Just because you should hold onto financial records for your reference doesn't mean you need to keep them forever. Different kinds of documents can be removed from your filing system at different times. For example, as previously mentioned, documents that are only used for your tax returns can be safely discarded three years after filing the return in nearly all cases. You may only need to keep other documents around for a year or, in some cases, just a few months if it's something you don't need to reference again. We'll look at how long you should keep various kinds of records later on in this chapter. Getting rid of documents you no longer need will help you cut down on clutter and make it easier to find the files you're actually looking for.

Many documents can be replaced whenever you get a new, updated version. For example, if you receive an annual investment statement, you can safely get rid of the quarterly or monthly ones you had before as long as you've already made any necessary quarterly tax payments. If you have an updated insurance policy, you can toss the old one, since it's no longer applicable for you. The same strategy applies to more mundane documents like recycling pickup schedules and flyers for events that have passed. Keeping these documents around just adds to the clutter around the office. For documents without private information, you can simply throw these papers away. Anything with information that only your company can access, or anything with financial records you no longer need to keep, should be shredded.

Don't forget to clear out your digital records as well. Your computer can get just as cluttered with old files you haven't touched in years as your physical filing cabinets can. Set aside some time at least once a year to go through all your files, digital and physical, and throw away or shred anything you no longer need. The more frequently you do this, the less work it will be, so you can perform this review on a biannual or quarterly basis if you prefer.

Schedule Regular Monthly Meetings

Though your monthly budget is primarily based on the average income and expenses of previous months, it can still fluctuate. This is especially true for new businesses, where expansion occurs more often and where relatively small surprise expenses can seriously shake up your finances before you have enough money saved up to cover them. Since your situation is likely to change throughout the year, schedule periodic check-ins to make sure you and your financial team are aware of these changes and you're all working together to adjust your plan accordingly. Hold monthly meetings to ensure nothing falls by the wayside, so you can continue to stay organized with your records and your finances as a whole.

How Long to Keep Your Records

You can get rid of most records eventually, but tossing them too early can cause some issues. Here's a quick rundown of different kinds of documents commonly used in business accounting and how long you should keep them around.

In most cases, you won't need to refer back to financial records after three years have passed. However, if something is wrong with your tax return, or if the IRS suspects there may be foul play, they can ask to see documents for up to seven years after the tax return in question. If part of your tax return includes a claim of loss filed because of bad debt deduction or worthless securities, keep these records for seven years. If you fail to report some of your income and the missing income is more than 25% of the gross income you reported, keep your documents for six years. If you don't file a return, or your return is fraudulent, you'll likely have to keep these papers around forever. If you want to simplify this process a little, and you know you're not committing fraud, you can save everything for seven years, which is the maximum amount of time the IRS has to ask for these documents under normal circumstances. Keep any accounting services records for the full seven years. Also do this for operational records such as credit card statements, bank account statements, canceled checks, and cash receipts

There are a few exceptions to this general rule, of course. Keep your business tax returns and supporting records for three years, as mentioned previously. If there's a chance you could have made a substantial error on your taxes, you should keep these records around for six years instead, as the IRS may try to correct the issue. Various types of employee information documents have different lengths of time where they can be questioned as well. You should keep employment tax records for four years after the tax is paid or from when it's due, whichever of the two is later. Keep job applicant information for three years, even if you didn't end up hiring them. Maintain employee files for seven years after an employee leaves. Finally, if you have documents related to an employee claim such as severance, worker's compensation, or other legal issues, keep these for 10 years.

Records You Should Keep Forever

There are a few kinds of records you should never get rid of. This is true for tax information for years where you failed to file. Failure to file also includes years where you may have filed past the due date. If you have active contracts, such as lease agreements, stock certificates, and operation permits, keep these for as long as they remain active and up to date. You should also retain any ownership records related to the formation of the business and any relevant by-laws.

Where to Keep Your Records

You know what to keep, but now you need to know where you're going to put all these files. For the most part, your financial records are either private documents or forms you don't want to lose, so privacy and security are key points to consider. You want to store everything so it's easy to access, but also so that there's no risk of it going missing or getting damaged. You'll need to make similar considerations for how you store both physical and digital documents.

Physical Records

Storing your records physically means you have a paper copy of all your information that would be difficult to tamper with, but it also means you need to worry more about keeping these documents safe. They could be damaged through regular wear and tear from being left out, for example, you don't want to grab your new balance sheet and find it has a big coffee ring on it. Paperwork can also be damaged by accidents like office fires. You should focus on getting yourself out of the building if there's a fire, not running back in to grab some papers, so whatever storage method you choose should give you peace of mind just in case something like this occurs.

Many companies use fire-resistant filing cabinets for exactly this reason. On the off chance that a fire does break out in the office, your records will be safe. Using a filing cabinet comes with the added benefit of allowing for easy storage. Use hanging folders and label each folder with different types of documents, dates, or however else you choose to organize your records. In lieu of a filing cabinet, you can also use a safe or a safe deposit box. Most safes are fire-resistant, and they also offer greater security for private documents. You can rent a safe deposit box from your bank, usually on an annual basis. The downside to safes and safe deposit boxes is that you may have trouble organizing or storing many files due to their smaller size, so reserve these for your most important documents that you don't have to access every day.

Digital Records

If you want to reduce clutter even further while still keeping your records as safe and organized as possible, you can store them digitally instead. Make scanned copies of all your files, as well as backups of these copies that you store on another device, like an external hard drive. This way, if your computer stops working, you'll still have access to all your files. Once you have everything scanned, don't forget to sort it into different folders so it's easy to find what you're looking for. You can set a password on any folders you want to restrict access to.

If you're looking for additional security, cloud service storage encrypts your files. These files are then stored remotely from your computer, so you can access them on any device. Just make sure the company you decide to use has a reliable reputation without a repeated history of data breaches so you can be sure your information is in the right hands.

A Step-by-Step Record Keeping System

A good record-keeping system needs to be reliable, efficient, practically automatic, well-organized, and easy to retrieve information when you need to. For many, the solution to this puzzle is as simple as an expanding file folder. You can organize your paperwork inside the folder, then store it in a filing cabinet, safe, or safe deposit box for additional protection. If you stick to this method, adding up your income and expenses at the end of the month will be a breeze, which means accounting will take as little time as possible while still being accurate.

Step 1: Set Up Your Folder

Start with your expanding file folder and use some labels. Each pocket of the folder should be labeled with a different type of income or expense. Group all your income sources on one end of the folder, and all your expenses on the other. It's best to use labels that can be easily removed rather than writing directly on the folder itself so you can always change the categories or add another if your situation changes. In a pinch, a small piece of masking tape can serve as a label that can be easily peeled off and replaced.

Step 2: Categorize

Each time you have to store a record that belongs to one of the categories you've created, simply retrieve the expanding file folder and drop it in the corresponding pocket. If you want to make things even easier on yourself in the future, organize the papers in each pocket by date so you don't have to sort through them later. File records right away; don't leave them around and hope someone else will put them away later, as more often than not you'll forget about the document entirely and you won't have any idea where it ended up when you really need it.

Step 3: Perform the Monthly Round-Up

At the end of each month, go through each pocket and add up your totals for the different categories of income and expenses. As you go, you can also add these totals to your monthly balance sheet. Each time you count up everything in a single pocket, write it down or use a calculator with register tape. Label this paper with the date, then staple everything together so the date label is right on top. You can now return this bundle to the folder and keep adding to it next month, as the stapled papers you've already added up are separated from the new records. Continue using the folder as you did before. At the end of the quarter, you should have three separate neat bundles of records in each pocket. At the end of the year, you'll have twelve, and you can easily identify which records are from which month at a glance. This makes doing your quarterly and annual taxes a snap.

Step 4: Check Your Odometer

If you want to ensure your calculations for your cost per mile are as accurate as possible, make a point to check your odometer at the start of each new load. Once you've finished the load, you can use the difference in miles to figure out your cost per mile for every trip. Store this information in your folder as well so you can easily reference it.

Step 5: Create Your Reports

Now that you have all the information you need, creating your monthly reports should take no time at all. Just look back through your folder and use the well-organized stacks of monthly revenue and expense records to fill out the parts of each financial statement. Better yet, use accounting software, which can do the calculation part for you and provide you with an easy-to-use template for many different forms. Once you have your financial statements, you can start analyzing them and creating your budget for next month.

Checklist and CDL Minded Approach

Keeping accurate, well-organized records is an invaluable practice for any CDL business. The more efficiently you keep track of all your expenses and sources of income, the easier it will be for you to identify any problem areas and adjust your business practices before they become issues that could affect the long-term success of your business.

To ensure you're tracking your finances in accordance with the tenets of the CPS, you can track your progress with the following checklist:

Task	Example	Complete?
Designate a place in your office for all records	Filing cabinet	
Choose a cloud storage service where you can upload all your files	Microsoft OneDrive	
Use folders, labels, and envelopes to organize your records	Create a designated folder for paid invoices	
Set up reminders for regular recording and organizing of your files	Set an alarm in your phone's calendar app for the first of each month	

CHAPTER 5

The Clutter Proof System— Keeping Your Business Running

Tracking your finances is just one part of staying fiscally healthy as a business. The other key component is how you analyze your income and spending history, and how you use this analysis to make smarter business decisions.

If you want to stay in business, you'll need to at least break even with expenses and income. If you want to continue to grow your business and turn it into a real success, you'll need to turn a profit. You can't do this if your spending is out of control, no matter how much money you make. Similarly, if you're not making enough money to cover even your fixed expenses, there's little chance your business will make it. The tricky part is that you'll need to balance your income and your expenses all while remaining competitive with other CDL companies in your area and offering affordable prices to customers. To thread this needle successfully, you'll need to carefully manage your costs, create and follow a solid payment collection strategy, and use various methods of financing to your advantage, at least until you've built up enough experience and goodwill to stand on your own two feet as a company.

Financing

Financing is how you fund your business operations outside of the money you make from customers. A well-established trucking company will have plenty of customers and jobs as well as multiple drivers to complete many jobs at the same time, which guarantees a steady flow of income. New companies aren't as well-known, and they don't attract as many customers as a result. You may not yet have the capital to grow your business just yet. In fact, you might be a business of one right now. Every company started out like this at some point, even the companies regarded as giants in their respective industries today.

Luckily, sales aren't the only method you have available to you for funding your business. You can also finance your company through the use of factoring, bank loans, and merchant cash advances.

Factoring

When you book a new job for your company, you don't necessarily get paid right away. You might not even get paid as soon as the order is complete, as some customers may take anywhere from 30 to 90 days to actually get you your payment. Meanwhile, you take on many expenses from the job that you have to pay immediately or within the month to avoid late fees. How can you afford to pay for the fuel you're using on a job you haven't been paid for?

The answer lies in factoring. Factoring "allows a business to obtain immediate capital or money based on the future income attributed to a particular amount due on an account receivable or a business invoice" (Barone, 2020, para. 3) through specific factoring companies. In other words, you can get the money for the job right away, minus the fees of the factoring company, in exchange for the full amount of the revenue you would have made on the job. You can think of factoring as a similar process to payday loans, though factoring companies generally lack the predatory practices that make payday loans so damaging to your finances. You don't have to pay the loan back, since the factoring company purchased your invoice in its entirety. You only need to pay the small associated fee.

Factoring can greatly improve your cash flow, as you get access to funds much faster than you would otherwise. The factoring company purchases your current invoices, and you get paid for them within 24 hours. They will then handle collecting payment from your customers. The factoring company will take their cut of the total invoice amount and give you the remainder. You can then use this cash to handle and complete customers' orders, pay employees, and take on more business as you continue to expand the company over time.

Keep in mind that the fees associated with factoring can vary based on your location and the company you're using. These fees are "usually between 1.5% and 3.5% for each receivable," (Schneider, 2020, para. 5), and while these are fairly low, they can add up if you're continually losing a small chunk of each invoice. That said, factoring comes with two big benefits that are hugely beneficial for small CDL companies and owner-operators. The first is that you no longer have to worry about chasing down your customers for payment on their invoices. This is now the factoring company's job, and you're free to focus on driving. The second is that you can ensure your business is getting a steady stream of revenue as long as you are taking and fulfilling new orders.

Factoring Mistakes You Must Avoid

Though factoring can be very helpful for your business, it can also become a problem if you're not careful. Common mistakes like failing to read all the terms, and the fine print of the agreement you make with the factoring company, can mean you're caught off-guard by them. Each company has its own fees and other policies you must agree to, so you should carefully review these before engaging in any factoring.

Additionally, make sure your customers are paying the factoring company, not you. If they pay you in cash when you complete the order or you receive a check or electronic payment from them, forward this money to the factoring company. Otherwise, you are violating the terms of the agreement and this can be seen as purposeful fraud, even if you simply didn't notice your mistake. This is yet another reason why keeping track of your revenue and good record-keeping, in general, is so important.

Don't forget to fully vet the factoring company before you agree to use them. While many factoring companies operate exactly as advertised, there are plenty of people looking to make a quick buck on unsuspecting business owners. You don't want to end up scammed out of your money, so look for factoring companies with good reviews and positive histories that don't involve any major scandals.

You should also avoid making factoring the singular source of income for your business. While it can help you get on your feet, you don't want to constantly be losing part of your income to factoring companies. Also, if something goes wrong and you are no longer able to use factoring, either because your business doesn't qualify, or because the factoring company closes, your only revenue source will dry up and you'll have to figure out how to process collections yourself without any warning. It's better to work your way off of relying on factoring slowly as your company continues to grow and to supplement it with other income sources like bank loans and cash advances.

Make sure you're picking the right kind of factoring for you and your customers as well. Both recourse and non-recourse factoring are available. With recourse factoring, if your customer doesn't pay their invoice balance to the factoring company within the agreed-upon time period, you will become responsible for paying it in full. You are essentially buying the invoice back, and you will have to seek payment from the customer yourself. With non-recourse factoring, if a customer doesn't pay, the factoring company writes off the expense and they don't come after you for it. This is the best option if you're worried your customers won't pay, but you'll also pay higher fees on non-recourse factoring since the factor has to take on a higher level of risk. The right option for you depends on how reliable you believe your customers are.

Less reliable customers will make it nearly impossible to use factoring successfully. If your customers don't pay the invoice within the allotted time, which can be up to 120 days from the original purchase, this can cost you if you're using recourse factoring. If you're worried about their reliability, you might opt for non-recourse factoring instead, which will cost you more in fees. Either way, unreliable customers cause you to lose money, so be careful about which customers you're working with.

Finally, some companies make the mistake of creating their quotes without considering the factoring fee. If you charge the same price as a regular order, but two or three percent gets taken by the factoring company, you'll be making fewer profits. If you adjust your invoices to account for these fees appropriately, however, this shouldn't be a problem.

Asset-Based Lending

Most banks are hesitant to give new companies loans without collateral because if your business goes bankrupt, they don't have any way to make back their money. Since you won't have an extensive history, or a full savings account when you're just starting out, banks consider you a risk. To counteract this, you can apply for an asset-based loan or revolving line of credit, where you put up a valuable asset as collateral.

You can use equipment, vehicles, and other high-value assets owned by your company as collateral for these loans. You can also use your accounts receivables. Just keep in mind that if you cannot pay back your loan, or if you fall too far behind on your credit payments, the bank can and will repossess these assets. Avoid using personal assets to secure loans for your company, as you might lose your business and another high-value possession, like your car or house at the same time. Remember that if your company is an LLC or another type of business that separates your finances and debts from those of your company, you don't have to use your personal funds to repay debts incurred by your business. It is safer to only secure these loans with business assets.

Asset-based loans charge interest until you can pay back all of what you owe. This interest is charged as an annual percentage rate (APR) that can "range from 7% to 15%" (Commercial Capital LLC, n.d., para. 13) depending on factors like the size of the loan or credit limit and how risky the transaction is from the bank's perspective.

Merchant Cash Advance

Merchant cash advance (MCA) providers function similarly to factors. Just like in factoring, you can secure an advance that is paid out to you immediately based on the funds you expect to have in the future. Unlike factoring, the company doesn't buy the invoice from you. Instead, with an MCA, the cash advance becomes a loan you have to pay back. You will need to pay interest on it, just like any other loan, and the rates for MCAs are usually higher than factoring fees and asset-based lending rates. While you will make installment payments on the loan, interest can build up quickly if you let the cash advance go unrepaid for too long.

Unlike some other loans, MCAs are specifically designed for businesses, so their repayment method is a little unique. When you take out the loan, you agree to pay the MCA provider a certain percentage of all daily credit card sales. MCAs are popular with retail stores and restaurants that perform many credit card transactions in a day, as this allows them to pay off their cash advances quickly and avoid large amounts of interest. You may find it harder to pay an MCA back because of your overall lower volume of orders per day and the fact that a smaller percentage of your customers will be placing orders on credit. That said, the requirements to qualify for an MCA are much lower than the other two financing methods we've previously discussed. Since your business is just starting out and it won't have an extensive credit history, you'll typically have a far easier time securing an MCA. You just need to make sure you have a system in place to pay it back.

No matter which financing method you use, if any, it's important to keep your business' credit in good standing. Pay off your debt as soon as you can. If possible, avoid maintaining a balance on company credit cards, and strive to pay them off in full every month. Not only will this reduce the amount of interest you'll pay overall, but it will also ensure your business qualifies for better loans and insurance rates when you apply for these in the future.

Collection

If you complete five orders but none of the customers for those orders have paid their invoices yet, you haven't made any money. Worse, you're actually in debt, since you had to spend money on fuel and other supplies to complete these jobs, as well as employee salaries, if applicable. This is why you need a good routine collection system. Without collecting on your invoices, you won't have any cash flow, even if you're doing a lot of business.

Cash flow problems are a leading cause of business failure, especially in the CDL industry where you make all your money from invoices that may not get paid until months after the actual job. Securing customers isn't enough to be successful. You must also have a strategy for getting customers to pay what they owe so you can minimize the wait time between sending an invoice and receiving payment. Your billing strategy, especially for chronically late payers, will be a huge determining factor in whether your business sinks or swims in its first few years.

There are plenty of ways you can encourage customers to pay you back in a reasonable amount of time that are far more persuasive than just asking for the money. Some people prefer to play hardball with their customers, not letting them place new orders while they still have unpaid ones, or charging interest on overdue debts, but this isn't your only option either, nor should it necessarily be the first one you resort to. This can put customers in a bad mood and discourage them from using your services again in the future. Instead, try to tempt your customers into agreeing to pay earlier by offering certain benefits if they do. For example, you could have a policy where if they pay their invoice within a slightly shorter payment period, they get a small discount in exchange. It's more than worth the couple of dollars you're giving up to have your money now rather than later, especially if you're having cash flow issues.

This method is also effective because it gives customers a choice in how they want to pay, which makes them feel like more of an active participant. If they choose to pay you back sooner for the discount, they'll feel more inclined to actually follow through. If they choose to forego the discount and pay a little later, they'll still likely try to pay sooner than they would otherwise because they chose the longer repayment term. This may not work with all of your customers, but it should help you receive faster payments from most of them.

Be Selective About Customers

Unfortunately, there are just some customers who are chronically late making payments no matter what you do. They may have significant financial burdens that prevent them from keeping up with all their expenses, especially if you're delivering them supplies for their own business. You might assume that there's no way to know this without actually working with these customers first, but actually, this information is available to anyone if you perform a credit check on their company before agreeing to work with them.

You can instantly check a company's credit online through services like Creditsafe and Experian. Credit scores above about 690 are generally considered good, while those below 630 are considered poor. You should be cautious about working with companies that have poor or bad credit, as this implies they've had trouble paying off their debts before. Newer companies may also have lower credit scores because there is no extensive credit history available, but if a company is making all of its payments on time, it really shouldn't have a credit score that dips below good or fair. If a business has bad credit, you might opt not to offer them credit at all, requiring that you're paid up-front or that you collect the money when you drop off their order instead. You can also simply choose not to work with them at all.

It's okay to be selective about who you decide to work with. It can feel like you're leaving money on the table by rejecting potential customers, especially when you're just starting out, but the truth is that customers who never repay you, or who seriously hamper your cash flow, aren't the right fit for your business. You'll rack up too many expenses delivering their orders and having nothing to show for it for months. It's okay to decide you don't want to work with a company that has an exceptionally poor credit history, or one where you've made deliveries in the past and had too much trouble getting them to pay up. It's a tough call, but ultimately one you must make for the long-term health of your business.

Lay Out Your Terms Clearly

If you agree to do business with a customer, make sure your terms are clear and fully understood. If someone misinterprets when they owe you payment, or how much they owe, this can delay the collection process even further. It's best to keep everything in writing so customers can refer back to the agreement you made when they agreed to work with your company. If there are any disagreements between you and the customer, checking the written terms and conditions can clear up most disputes. If you ever reach a point where collecting payment from a customer becomes a legal issue, you'll have a much better chance of proving your case if you can show they signed a contract for each job. The clearer you can make your terms, the more likely it is that customers will follow them, and the better you'll be able to defend yourself if they don't.

Forge Long-Term, Personal Relationships

Let's say you owe $100 in credit card debt and $100 to a close friend of yours. Who do you feel most obligated to pay back first? Chances are, even though your friend might not charge you interest, you'll instinctively want to make them the priority because you don't want to put them in a tough spot. You've talked face to face, and you know and care about each other. You don't necessarily have to become good friends with your customers, but you should strive to create personal relationships so they see you as a person, not a company. If they get to know you, not just your trucking business, they're more likely to make repaying you a priority.

Being friendly with your customers also increases the likelihood they'll place an order with your company again in the future. Try to interact face to face with repeat customers and treat them like you would want to be treated if you were in their shoes. Be friendly and fair, but not overly lenient, and customers will treat you with the same respect while also placing many future orders with you.

Managing Costs

If you want to reduce the burden of expenses and improve your cash flow, you need to keep your costs down. Look at where you're spending your money, as well as what sort of return you're getting on your investments. If you're spending hundreds or thousands of dollars on areas of your business that aren't generating much if any income, it's time to rework your strategy and trim these wasteful costs. Focus on the investments that help you grow your business the most.

Cost Per Mile

Your cost per mile is the amount of money you spend on expenses like food, gas, sleeping accommodations, and wages for each mile you or one of your employees drives. It's the standard for evaluating jobs to see whether they're worth the return on investment. If a job doesn't pay very well but you have to drive cargo halfway across the country, you're probably spending more on your expenses than you're actually making for the job, or at the very least your profits are very thin. Calculating your cost per mile can help you choose orders that are worth the time and money you spend on them.

When calculating cost per mile, make sure to account for all expenses and all miles driven during the trip. Check the odometer to keep your mileage records as accurate as possible. When adding up your expenses start with fixed costs like insurance, equipment, license and registration, cell phone service, software, and regular operational expense payments. Then add in variable costs, including maintenance, fuel, and road expenses. As for miles, remember that your loaded miles and empty miles will have a different impact on your cost per mile, as loaded trucks use up more fuel. You're only getting paid for loaded miles, so you should be primarily concerned with the cost per mile when the truck is loaded.

You can calculate your cost per mile for an individual trip, but you can also calculate it on a monthly basis. Just add up all monthly expenses and compare them to the total number of miles you drove during the month. This will show you whether you're making a net positive amount of money or a net negative, in which case you may need to be choosier about the kind of jobs you're accepting.

Fuel Prices

You might assume that the fuel that's listed at the cheapest pump price is the most cost-effective option. This might be true for regular drivers, but since the IFTA requires you to pay tax on the fuel you use during your journey, this might not be the case. Instead, you should choose the fuel with the lowest base price.

When you own a CDL business and pay fuel taxes, you're not paying the tax of the state where you get the fuel. The taxes you pay each time you refuel are credited to your account. Your tax is determined by your miles driven and average fuel mileage, calculated and paid, or refunded, on a quarterly basis. To figure out what the cheapest base price is, take the price of fuel and subtract the cost of taxes.

You can also reduce fuel costs by making small adjustments to increase your vehicles' gas mileage. Just little things like limiting your idling time, keeping tires at the right pressure, reducing your speed, making slow and gradual accelerations and decelerations, and sticking to your route can make a big difference. You can also make adjustments to the vehicle itself like adding a roof fairing, using larger dual fuel tanks so you can stock up on more fuel and stop less often, and using aluminum wheels or low-rolling-resistance tires. You might consider adding a fuel surcharge to your customers' bills or taking advantage of fuel optimization software to cut your costs even further.

Intangible Costs

Not all costs are reported on your tax returns. There are other intangible factors that can impact how much money you make, such as morale and the general attitude of you and your employees. Bad attitudes can make the workplace feel hostile. This drives away current and potential employees alike, it also puts everyone in a worse mood. Productivity can suffer and you might get in arguments with customers more often. You don't want to lose anyone's business because you were in a bad mood, or you didn't feel motivated to do your job, so try to keep the workplace as positive as possible. Small businesses with high employee morale are often more successful.

Overexpansion

Growth is generally considered a good thing, but not when you're attempting to expand past the boundaries of your niche. First, it's important to have a solid foundation that generates reliable income before you try to expand at all. If you do want to expand, stick to expansions that make sense for your type of company. For example, if you own a garbage truck business, it makes sense to purchase another truck and hire some more employees so you can expand your radius of service. It doesn't make sense for you to start offering interstate trucking services. This is out of your wheelhouse, and the customer base you've already built up doesn't have any reason to try out your new services. Avoid making unnecessary expansions into different niches that won't help you make more money. They will only detract from the time you have available to focus on your original business.

Maintenance

If you put off doing any maintenance on your vehicles until they start breaking down, you'll end up paying a lot more for repairs than you would if you had made smaller routine repairs. Regular maintenance cuts down on costs and ensures your vehicles are always in optimal shape. You won't have to lose a whole day of income because you had to send a truck for extensive repairs either. This also means they're less likely to break down on the side of the road, and drivers are less likely to get in a dangerous accident. Keep up with repairs in order to reduce your overall maintenance expenses and ensure your company is a safe place to work.

Transportation Management Systems

A transportation management system (TMS) is a program specifically designed for business owners in the CDL industry. It allows you to automate your IFTA reporting, manage loads and drivers, and simplify the payroll process. If you can reduce the amount of time you spend on routine office tasks, you can better allocate your time while also reducing your tax burden.

Cargo Protection

Loss of cargo can cut into your profits, whether it's the result of an accident on the road or someone stealing cargo out of the back of the truck. Go over common loss prevention strategies with all your drivers. Ensure cargo is properly tied down and secured before getting in the truck. Follow all safety protocols on the road. When drivers stop to eat and sleep, their trucks should be locked with no access to the cargo. Taking these easy preventative measures cuts down on cargo loss, so you can make more money and keep customers happy.

Plan Your Routes

Planning both your route and your stopping points ahead of time can save you a lot of trouble when you're on the road. It might be tempting to just punch an address into a GPS and get in the truck, but taking a little extra time to research where you're going, and the best way to get there, is worth the extra effort. You can choose the most efficient route that has conveniently spaced stops so you'll never find yourself driving around in the dead of night looking for somewhere to stay the night without any luck.

Checklist and CDL Minded Approach

Reducing your expenses will help you stay in business for years to come. Perform regular reviews of your profit and loss statements as well as your budgets to see where you can shore up your profits and eliminate excessive spending.

Follow this checklist to eliminate expenses the CDL Minded way:

Task	Where to Find Resources	Complete?
Research factoring companies with good terms so you have a backup plan for issues with cash flow and collection	BlueVine, eCapital, Fundbox	
Find credit agencies/bureaus for background checks on potential clients	TransCredit, RTS Financial, Experian	
Take a hard look at your expenses and see where you can cut the fat	Review your financial statements, speak to your accountant	
Set reminders for routine preventative maintenance on all company vehicles	Write reminders in your calendar	
Find gas stations on your route with the cheapest base price, not pump price, and buy gas there	TruckMaster Fuel Finder, Fuelbook, Trucker Path	

CHAPTER 6

All About Taxes

You are obligated to pay taxes to the government for any income your company makes, as well as for certain purchases. Taxes are serious, and making a mistake knowingly or unknowingly could have significant negative repercussions for your business. Your CPA will guide you through complicated tax laws so you can save as much money as possible, but it's still important for you to know the basics so you can be involved in this process.

Applicable Business Taxes

You are responsible for paying multiple different taxes on your own income, as well as the income of your business. Make sure you file both your federal and state taxes every year.

Business Federal Income Taxes

If your company turns a profit, you'll have to pay federal income taxes on that profit. The rate and method for filing varies depending on the business model. For corporations whose profits are taxed separately, the tax rate is 21% as of the 2017 Tax Cuts and Jobs Act (Tax Policy Center, 2020, para. 1). Other small business models, like LLCs and sole proprietorships, have the company's profits lumped into their own income for tax time. In this case, you only need to file one federal tax return, and you'll only have to pay self-employment tax rates on both your and the company's income.

Self-Employment Taxes

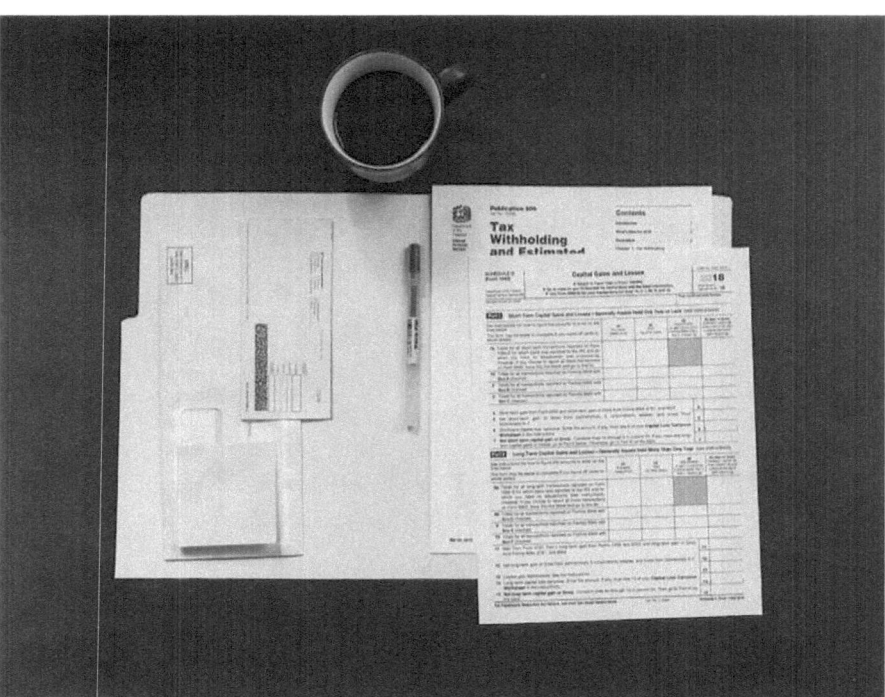

Business owners are considered to be self-employed under tax law. Since you don't have an employer who will send you a W-2 at the end of the year, you'll need to keep track of your income yourself. Your taxes include Medicare and Social Security payments based on the net income of your business, as well as any other income sources you might have. These taxes account for about 15.3% of your income minus deductions.

You can ease the burden of tax time by making quarterly estimated payments. Since you don't fill out a W-2, these quarterly payments function as your withholdings. If you expect you'll owe at least $1,000 in federal taxes, you're required to make quarterly payments to avoid a late fine. Calculate these estimated payments with a Form 1040-ES, which you can find on the IRS website.

Sales Tax

If your business operates in any states that have sales taxes, you must factor this into your business. Include sales tax on the invoices you send to customers, but remember that sales tax rates can vary between states and some might not have any sales tax at all. Customers should only pay the sales tax of their state, not your company's home base. Collect the money to cover this tax, then report and pay it on your state taxes.

Gross Receipts and State Income Taxes

A gross receipts tax is a tax on your business' revenues. It can replace regular state income taxes, or you may need to pay both. Check your state's laws to see if this applies to you, and if it does, make sure to file these appropriately.

Applicable Taxes for Trucking and Transportation Businesses

Some taxes are only applicable to businesses in the transportation industry, so make sure not to forget them if you're using tax filing software that might not ask if they're applicable, or if your accountant doesn't have much experience with trucking companies. These are the heavy-highway vehicle use tax and IFTA fuel tax returns. Make sure you're tracking your related income and expenses throughout the year so you don't have to go searching through piles of old records to find the necessary information.

Heavy-Highway Vehicle Use Tax

The heavy-highway vehicle use tax (HVUT) is a tax imposed on heavy vehicles that use public roads regularly, such as the tractor-trailers or other large commercial vehicles your company might use. The tax is used to support infrastructure development and repair, keeping roads properly maintained, and funding safety programs like vehicle inspection and government-run driving schools.

Not all CDL companies need to pay HVUT. It's only applicable for vehicles with a gross weight of at least 55,000 pounds. To calculate a truck's gross weight to see if you need to pay this tax, add together the unloaded weight of the truck, the unloaded weight of any attached trailers, and the maximum weight of the loads you use the truck to carry.

HVUT is collected on a yearly basis. To remain compliant with tax laws, if you need to pay it, you must fill out a 2290 tax form and submit it to the IRS along with payment, which will vary based on the weight of your vehicle, up to a maximum of $550.

IFTA Fuel Tax Returns

We've already discussed the necessity of paying fuel taxes and how the IFTA applies to CDL businesses, so as long as you remember to pay it on a quarterly basis you should have no issues. You can pay this tax with the Department of Revenue's IFTA Fuel Tax System. The website also lets you request additional IFTA tags for other vehicles. If you want to make paying this tax as easy as possible, use IFTA reporting software, which will quickly tell you how much you owe.

Tax Deductions

Don't underestimate the power of tax deductions. Ignoring potential deductions is leaving money on the table, so you should go through each possible option relevant to CDL companies and determine if it's applicable for your business. Deductions reduce your amount of taxable income and lower your owed taxes in return, but they're not tax credits, which directly reduce your required payment. Remember that a deduction of $100 doesn't mean that you'll pay $100 less in taxes. It just means $100 of your earned income won't be included when calculating how much you owe. This is why it's so important to take advantage of as many deductions as possible.

Here's a list of deductible expenses that might apply to your business:

- Start-up costs

- Truck lease payments

- Permits and license fees

- Computer software

- Accounting services

- Administrative fees, such as those from ATMs and check reorders

- Business interest expenses

- Repairs and accessories

- Association dues

- Postage fees

- Cleaning and office supplies

- Utilities, such as internet, cell phone, and electricity

- Real estate expenses, such as penalties and related taxes

- Subscriptions related to trucking and business ownership

Some deductible expenses have additional rules attached. For example, you can deduct per diem expenses, which include the total cost of meals and drinks you or your drivers purchased while completing a job, including the tip. However, you can only deduct 80% of these expenses.

You can also take a deduction for depreciation of company assets, and you have a few options. You can take the whole deduction upfront if each individual asset you're claiming costs less than $2,500, rather than taking a smaller depreciation payment each year. This gets you your money upfront, but it means you can't take another deduction for depreciation next year. This is better for items that lose their value quickly and cheaper purchases, as well as situations where you're less financially well-off now than you would be in future years, as is often the case with new businesses.

What You Can't Deduct

While there are plenty of business expenses that are tax-deductible, there are also many that cannot be deducted. These include expenses that are related to your personal life rather than your company, such as your home phone line, personal vacations, time spent working on non-company equipment, downtime, and the interest paid on any personal loans. For devices like your home phone and non-company computers, you cannot deduct these because they aren't exclusively used for work purposes. You also can't deduct any lost income from unpaid mileage or deadheading, which are trips where you aren't carrying any cargo or passengers. Additionally, while fuel costs you accrue on the job have their own set of rules with the IFTA, any personal commuting costs like gas, tolls, or parking fees cannot be deducted either.

Schedule of Payment of Taxes

Paying your taxes on time is mandatory. Whether you only have to submit your tax return in April or you're also making quarterly payments throughout the year, missing a deadline means paying late fees. Make sure you pay your self-employment and income quarterly taxes by the end of each fiscal quarter if you expect you will owe at least

$1,000 in taxes for the year, minus credits and withholding. The fiscal quarters are three month periods from January 1st to March 31st, April 1st to May 31st, June 1st to August 31st, and September 1st to December 31st. Quarterly payments are due on April 15, June 15, September 15, and January 18 of the following year, respectively. Note that despite these periods being called quarters, they're not actually equal lengths of time, so you'll have to plan accordingly, and your payments may not all be the same during a single year.

If you're having trouble setting aside enough money for quarterly payments, or you tend to forget to pay before the due date, you can make monthly payments instead. Many people find this easier, as you're spending less money at a time even if the total amount you pay doesn't change. Make sure you pay before the 15th of each month if you're using this method so you won't miss the quarterly deadlines. With this method, you can budget for quarterly payments on a monthly basis just like other expenses.

Getting Help With Taxes

Taxes can be very confusing from a layperson's perspective, not to mention time-consuming. If you want to let the experts handle the tricky parts and free up more time for yourself, there are plenty of ways you can find someone to assist with your taxes. We've already discussed the benefits of hiring a CPA, who can prepare your taxes for you, but there are many other resources at your disposal as well.

Tax preparation software like TurboTax and H&R Block can help guide you through some of the more complex tax considerations. These services make calculations for you, so you only need to plug in the right numbers. You can also file your taxes right away online, sending an electronic payment, or getting a mailed check, or convenient direct deposit for your refund. Some services are even specifically geared toward business owners. However, these programs don't offer advice and support specific to the trucking industry, so they might not be your best option if you need more guidance.

Many companies provide tax consultations specifically for trucking businesses and CDL holders for a nominal fee. They can prepare your taxes for you or guide you through the preparations while suggesting the best deductions. These companies may also provide trucking-specific accounting services for year-round use. Options include eTruckerTax, TruckerTaxes.com, Transportation Accounting Services, and Larsen & Associates. Look into these and other companies that offer these services and figure out their usual fees before you decide if they're a good fit for your needs.

Other Tips to Minimize Taxes

To make sure you're paying as little as possible while still complying with the law, pick a tax assistance method that fits your current situation. Some companies offer services geared toward owner-operators, while others can help you manage taxes for multiple drivers and additional employees.

You can reduce your taxable income and save at the same time by contributing to a retirement account such as an IRA, 401(k), or SEP. These accounts let you make tax-exempt deposits. You won't have to pay taxes until you start withdrawing from them. For most people, this is a better deal in the long run, as your lower income when you're retired will put you in a lower tax bracket. It's also a smart move to prioritize saving for retirement at any age, so don't forget to make regular contributions.

Even though you can't deduct personal vehicle miles from your commute to and from work, you can deduct miles if they're for trips related to doing business, even if they're in your personal vehicle. If you make a trip to a parts store, supply store, meeting, the bank your business holds an account with, or a truck show, you can deduct the relevant expenses, so keep track of these miles in a notebook in your car each time you make one of these trips.

If you have kids who are interested in the business, consider employing them for age-appropriate jobs. While only people 18 or older can get a CDL, and driving across state lines requires that you're at least 21, teens can still work in a family-owned business. Not only does this give them work experience and their own source of income, but it also helps you save money on taxes. If you pay your kids about $4,000 a year for their work, they won't pass the threshold where they have to pay taxes on that income, and you won't have to pay tax on it either. Note that even though you're hiring your kids, which means they can work at a younger age, you still need to follow child labor laws, which limit how long they can work and what jobs they can do without endangering their safety. Ensure your kids also have enough free time to complete their homework and that they're never allowed in areas where they could be injured.

If you or your college-aged kids are in school and paying tuition, you can deduct this as well in the form of tuition tax credits. In order to take advantage of this option, the college or university must be a qualified educational institution. A tuition tax credit can be as much as $2,500, which is directly applied to what you owe rather than your income like a deduction, so you don't want to leave this credit on the table. If your kids are a little older and you're making payments toward their student loans, you can deduct these interest payments instead.

As an important note, the more unusual your claimed expenses are, the more likely it is that this will attract the attention of the IRS and you will get audited. If you claim a substantially high number of expenses, especially those that are uncommon for the type and size of your business, you'll more than likely have to prove these claims with proper documentation. This is one reason of many why it's a good idea to have a licensed professional help you prepare your taxes. Even accidental tax fraud is still tax fraud, and you don't want to invite an audit if you can avoid it. If you keep your affairs in order, you should have no problem getting your quarterly tax payments and tax returns accepted, and you can easily verify any expenses that the IRS questions. Stick with the Clutter Proof System and it will save you an invaluable amount of time and stress during tax season.

Checklist and CDL Minded Approach

Taxes can be confusing when you're a business owner. You no longer only have yourself to worry about. You also need to keep track of the financial records for your business, record everything accurately, and take advantage of possible tax deductions and credits whenever they're available to you. Use all the resources you can to minimize the amount you are legally required to pay in taxes. Look at every potential deduction and see whether it applies to you. Even a credit of just a few dollars can add up with other deductions and make the extra time you spent reviewing your deductions completely worthwhile.

Follow this checklist for preparing your taxes the CDL Minded way:

Task	Tips	Complete?
Meet with your tax advisor or accountant and list out all the deductions you qualify for	Meet at least a month before tax day so you have time to gather information	
Set reminders in your calendar for all tax filing and payment deadlines	Add quarterly and annual deadlines as phone alarms	
Break down quarterly or annual tax payments into monthly expenses and include them in your budget	Estimate your yearly tax burden based on last year's taxes	
Keep a record of all the receipts and other proofs of payment you need for your deductions	Organize receipts into labeled folders	

CHAPTER 7

Preparing for the Future

When you're building a business from the ground up, all sorts of things can go wrong. A vehicle might break down at the worst possible time, putting a strain on you and your finances. You or another driver could get into an accident, getting hurt or damaging the cargo being shipped. There could be a big shakeup in the industry that changes the way the game is played, for better or for worse, and you'll need to find a way to adapt to these changes if you want your business to survive. In short, the future is uncertain, and there is always a risk that something will go wrong whether you see it coming or not.

Since not every emergency or big change can be predicted, it's important to be prepared for anything. Good preparation will help you survive any storm and keep all your finances in order, which minimizes the risk of your business having to shut its doors from a single unexpected expense. Everything you do now to brace for future hiccups protects your business. You can't know what will happen next for certain, but you can insulate yourself from it as much as possible if you allocate your money and time appropriately. Three key ways for your business to prepare for the future are setting aside enough money for an emergency fund; paying for up-to-date insurance on the business itself, the employees, and different aspects of transportation; and keeping an eye on the market so you have some forewarning when things look like they're going to change in a big way.

Emergency Fund

Everyone needs an emergency fund, even businesses. There's always a risk that something completely unexpected will happen that ends up monopolizing a significant portion of your income. Even if you can cover this expense, it will throw off your budget and leave you scrambling to make up the difference, which can strain your finances for many months after the original emergency. You don't want to turn a temporary expense into a major, long-lasting problem, and the best way to avoid this is to save enough money to pay off any surprise expenses as soon as they happen. To accomplish this, you'll need to set up an emergency fund for your business.

Unforeseen expenses can be especially dangerous for your business when you're still in the early stages. When you've been operating for many years, you'll naturally increase your income with fewer expenses, so handling emergencies isn't such a big deal. When you're just barely making enough to cover all your expenses, or when you're funneling most of your profits into growing your company, a sudden large expense could mean you aren't able to pay off your debts or keep up with your other expenses anymore. Fall too far into debt, and this will start to threaten your company.

If you have an emergency fund, however, you can avoid this problem entirely. You'll have enough money saved up to cover your bases, so you won't end up with mountains of debt. It's a great way to ensure you can continue to build your business without constantly feeling stressed over your finances. Additionally, your emergency fund will come in handy for months when you get less business than usual. Maybe you run a tour bus business, but one month there's a lot of snow, which keeps tourists away. You might have nearly the same amount of expenses, but less income to cover them with. If you have an emergency fund, you won't have any trouble making up the difference until warm weather returns.

For each month that your business makes a profit, set some money aside in a savings account. Use this account to steadily grow your emergency fund over time without restricting your ability to make other purchases for your business. Continue to contribute to the account until you have at least three to six months worth of business expenses. This ensures that even in a worst-case scenario, such as if you are ever sick or injured, and you can't work for multiple months, there is minimal risk of having to close your business before you can return to work. If you ever deplete your emergency fund, work to build it back up before you attempt to continue to grow your business so you always have some money saved up.

Insurance

You probably have your own health insurance coverage and maybe even a life insurance policy; you might have homeowner's or renter's insurance, and your car is also insured. Insurance helps you protect the things that are most valuable to you by covering the bills if an accident or emergency ever occurs. It only makes sense, then, that you should have insurance for your business as well. After all, you should be very passionate about your company and want to see it succeed no matter what bumps on the road you might encounter in the future.

One common argument against getting insurance is that the monthly or annual payments are too expensive for you to manage. Why diminish your profits even further than what start-up expenses have already reduced them to? This is an understandable concern, but the truth is that if something happens that would have been partially or completely covered by insurance but you failed to buy it, it's often far more costly to fix the problem when you have to pay out of your own pocket. More often than not, these accidents are more expensive than the cost of the insurance. Additionally, paying for insurance gives you peace of mind you might not have otherwise had. If you get in an accident, your first thought won't be about how much money repairing or replacing your truck is going to cost you. Instead, it will be about the safety of everyone involved, including yourself, which is a much more important consideration.

There are many different types of insurances that are necessary for CDL businesses. These include insurances for both business-related and transport-related accidents. With insurance, you have protection in case a customer is harmed by your business, physically or financially, and decides to sue. You can also buy insurance for natural disasters and other accidents that could destroy company property so you're reimbursed for the equipment cost. Protect your employees, the cargo you're hauling, and your business as a whole by taking the proactive step of getting insured.

Business-Related Insurance

If you have general liability insurance, you're protected in the event that an accident occurs where you're at fault and someone is hurt or their property is damaged. It assists in paying to replace damaged property, as well as any medical bills related to the incident. It can also cover administrative costs, court fees, and settlements that would otherwise place a significant financial burden on your company.

General liability insurance is required for all registered trucking businesses according to the FMCSA. This is because if you don't have this insurance, you might not be able to pay these claims if your company doesn't generate enough income. This means the person or entity suing for compensation wouldn't be able to get their money. In most cases, "you must carry at least $750,000 in primary liability coverage," but "many shippers and brokers require $1 million in liability coverage" (Getloaded, n.d., para. 11) depending on the situation. Ensure you pay for enough insurance coverage so you don't have to pay these costs yourself.

If you want to protect your business' assets, you'll need commercial property insurance. This is insurance that will pay some or all of the current value of any property that is lost or damaged from improper use, a fire, theft, or other causes. Commercial property insurance covers assets such as tools, equipment, inventory, personal property, the office building, and any furniture inside. However, it has its limitations. It does not cover items that were damaged intentionally. It also doesn't cover damage to vehicles from an accident. For this, you'll need auto insurance.

If you want to make business-related insurance as simple as possible, you can buy business owner's insurance. This combines different types of insurances into one simple bundle. This keeps things straight-forward so you know exactly what you're covered for and what you're not according to your individual policy. It also means you only have to pay one insurance bill rather than paying multiple from different companies, which keeps your budget from getting too cluttered. You can cover all your bases without getting caught up in specifics.

Transport-Related Insurance

In addition to business-related insurance, you'll also need to protect yourself while you're on the road. This starts with cargo insurance, which helps to cover any damages to loads. This is another type of insurance that is mandated by the FMCSA, but it's one you should want to have anyway, as it can save you thousands if there's an accident that destroys cargo, or if cargo is stolen from the truck. Typically, you'll want about $100,000 in coverage, but this varies based on what kinds of loads you're hauling. If you are routinely transporting more expensive cargo, you'll want to increase your insurance accordingly. Thankfully, more expensive cargo usually translates into better-paying jobs, so you shouldn't have much trouble covering your insurance fees.

Don't forget to protect your truck as well. Just like any other vehicle on the road, your truck can get damaged if it's in an accident. If you're not found liable for the accident, physical damage insurance can provide you with the funds you need to make the necessary repairs or buy a new truck.

Protecting the truck also means protecting the driver inside of it. You should have occupational accident insurance for yourself and all drivers working for you. Additionally, depending on the type of plan you get, this insurance may extend to passengers as well. Occupational accident insurance pays "medical, disability, death, and dismember-ment benefits for accidents that occur on the job," (Great American Insurance Group, n.d., para. 2) ensuring that no one is left injured without a way to pay for any necessary medical bills.

Some insurance plans help to cover the blind spots of standard physical damage insurance. For example, non-trucking insurance cov-ers accidents that occur when a truck is being driven for any purpose outside of business use. If you get in an accident on the way home from work, for example, non-trucking insurance will cover claims from the other party. You may also want to get bobtail insurance, which covers you if you're driving an unloaded truck and you're found to be liable for the accident. It won't pay for the damages to the truck, but it will help you pay costs associated with liability such as medical bills, legal fees, and settlement expenses.

Considerations When Choosing Insurance

Not every insurance plan is equal. Some offer better coverage, and some may be better fits for your price range. In many cases, you may not need the best insurance out there, but you should still do some shopping around to compare all of your options.

You can get insurance quotes without a hard credit check, which means there's no negative effect on your credit score. At the same time, having good credit may qualify you for better rates and premiums from some companies. Get quotes from multiple different insurance providers to see how these numbers stack up against each other, and look for companies that offer the benefits you need at a reasonable price for your credit level.

Consider how much coverage you actually need as well. If you're an owner-operator with no other drivers on your payroll, you probably don't need one of the more expensive coverage plans, as you only have to pay for coverage for yourself. If you employ many drivers, on the other hand, you'll need to find the insurance plan with the best value for multiple people. Drivers with plenty of experience and a clean record usually qualify for cheaper insurance, so keep this in mind during the hiring process.

Check the specific revenue cap regulations that apply to the insurance companies you're interested in as well. Many insurance plans have revenue caps, which limit the amount of money they can make from you that goes directly into their profits. Others have annual limit caps, which means they won't pay out more than a certain dollar amount in a year. A revenue cap usually works in your favor, though some insurance companies may simply increase the cost of claims. An annual limit cap always works against you as it is a hard limit on how much money an insurance company will provide, so opt for plans with higher annuals caps or track your expenses to make sure you're not in danger of reaching it yet.

Adjusting for Industry Changes

Every industry undergoes changes in market conditions throughout the years. A winning business strategy one year may become completely outdated five or six years down the line. If you don't make an effort to keep up with the times, you're going to have a very hard time keeping your business afloat in a highly competitive industry like trucking and other CDL jobs. Recognizing and making adjustments to accommodate industry changes is a necessary part of preparing for the future of your business.

Investing in Growth

Once you have a solid income-to-expense ratio, you should start look-ing for growth opportunities that don't put excessive strain on your budget. If you start out as an owner-operator, don't shy away from hiring employees when your revenue allows for it and you're getting enough business to warrant it. If you have only a small handful of employees and the work is becoming too demanding for them to han-dle, consider expanding your workforce so no one is stretching them-selves too thin and you don't have to reject job requests.

You can also try to increase both the area you service and the types of customers you attract. For a trucking business, this might look like accepting jobs in additional states or having some drivers get endorse-ments to haul specific types of cargo. For a Coach or shuttle bus busi-ness, this might mean expanding your fleet so you can cover more ground, or making more stops along the way to your destination to pick up more passengers.

Innovating and investing in your future isn't just important for rais-ing your profits. It also helps you attract the best possible employees. When you can offer competitive wages, and you clearly demonstrate your willingness to continue improving, you'll catch the interest of drivers who are looking for growth opportunities as well. This means your team is more motivated and driven as a whole, always looking to the future rather than getting stuck in the present, and they'll be will-ing to roll with industry changes just like you.

Track New Trends

As technology improves, the future landscape of CDL businesses will change. Currently, every truck needs a driver. However, in the future when self-driving cars become a common occurrence, this is likely to change. At some point, potentially in the near future, you may not need to have anyone inside a truck or bus at all to complete jobs. On one hand, this can make competition steeper, as this opens the playing field to just about everyone to run a commercial driving company, whether they have their own CDL or not. On the other hand, you may be able to use this to your advantage, cutting costs and focusing on spending your money on things other than driver salaries. You may be able to run your own autonomous fleet that practically runs the business for you, freeing up your time. Of course, you can only take advantage of this or deal with the potential negative repercussions if you actually pay attention to new trends.

It's also highly likely that trucks will move away from their reliance on fossil fuels and will instead become primarily or exclusively powered by electricity, especially as more emphasis is placed on environmentalism. Electric trucks could overhaul the way CDL companies deal with fuel, including IFTA taxes. This may also mean you have to spend money buying a whole new set of trucks as well. This transition will be especially costly if you wait until the switch is unavoidable, rather than buying one or two electric trucks every few years and spreading out the expenses.

While we are still a ways off from artificial intelligence (AI) and true machine learning, these factors may eventually play a role in how you run your trucking business as well. The better AI gets, the more refined self-driving vehicles will be, and the less face-to-face interaction will be necessary for completing each job. There's no real way to know how AI and machine learning will shape our future for certain, but these are important factors to consider and keep an eye on as you continue growing your business nevertheless.

Offer Employee Training

Remember that your employees are the core of your business, and when possible, it's better to retain your current employees than hire new ones all the time. If you need to start adapting to some upcoming trend or change, such as AI, make sure your employees are trained on what to expect and how to use any new technology you're utilizing for your business. This will make it easier for them to adapt, and having short but consistent training sessions will encourage your employees to look forward to change rather than fearing it. Every training session you offer your employees helps them expand their skill set, and become part of the next generation of drivers who are more than capable of handling new technologies and transportation models.

You can also work to improve employee experiences through the use of mobile technology. If your drivers aren't being given the tools they need to succeed, they'll start to feel less passion for their jobs, and they may not be interested in making the necessary changes to prepare for the future. Encourage your employees to stay connected with the company even when they're out on a job that puts them miles away so you can get data about arrival, departure, loading, and unloading, and wait times, as well as fuel and rest stops. As the use of technology continues to increase, it may be worth investing in the development of a custom-made app or website that allows employees to complete simple tasks like check-in with you at different milestones or request sick days all from their phone. If you insist on doing everything face-to-face, you may waste time and, consequently, money. Embrace new developments in technology and always consider how you can use them to improve the speed and efficiency of your business while also improving the average employee experience.

Analyze Road Data

Once you have data from your employees, analyze it and see what you can learn. Look at trends that contribute to increased wait times where no money is being made and see what you can do to reduce or eliminate them, whether this means selecting another route if drivers are waiting in traffic, or improving communication with the customer before the truck arrives so there's no delay for unloading. Continue collecting information with ELDs and apps so you can make consistent improvements to your business strategy and structure.

Checklist and CDL Minded Approach

As much as it might be tempting for things to remain the same once you've found a way to run your business that turns a profit, the truth is that future progress is inevitable. People will continue inventing new ways to complete old tasks and embracing more modern technologies throughout their daily lives. It is only by making a dedicated effort to keep up with these changes and to predict and prepare for whatever the future holds that you can keep your CDL business successful for years to come.

Use the following checklist to help you prepare for the future today:

Task	Tips	Complete?
Create an emergency fund for unexpected expenses.	If necessary, begin small and increase your contributions as you go	
Canvas for insurance quotes and research the right plan for your needs	Get quotes from companies like Progressive, The Hartford, and Nationwide	
Stay updated on the latest news in your market.	Sign up for an industry newsletter or Google alerts, or join an industry organization	

CONCLUSION

The number one reason businesses fail in any industry is poor financial management. If you're not putting in the effort to keep track of your spending so you can identify problem areas and course-correct before they threaten your business, you'll quickly find yourself overwhelmed by debt. If this is allowed to continue, which often happens because business owners simply don't know there even is a problem in the first place, it can threaten to ruin everything you've worked so hard to achieve in creating your own CDL company.

You can avoid this unfortunate fate and do your part to ensure your business has the best chance at success possible by staying on top of your finances. When you apply the contents of *CDL Minded Accounting* to your strategy for running your company and reviewing your finances, you'll find that it's easier than ever to keep an eye on your spending. Not only that, but you'll also be able to apply the Clutter Proof System to your business, so you'll never suffer from the effects of excessive clutter and disorganization again.

Throughout this book, you've learned skills that will assist you in becoming a better and more fiscally responsible business owner. You've learned about all the different registrations and permits necessary for your CDL business to operate. You understand essential bookkeeping and accounting terms and you can apply them when you create budgets and financial statements, all while avoiding common accounting mistakes. You've discovered how creating and sticking to a regular routine for storing financial documents in an organized way, whether they're physical or digital, will make things like payroll, budgeting, and tax time much easier for you. You've also learned how to ensure you remain in business for a long time to come by monitoring your spending, taking the appropriate tax deductions, and preparing for the future as much as you can. All you have to do now is apply these skills.

If you've always been very passionate about starting your own trucking company, now is the time to take the first step. You now have all the tools you need to not only start that business but also set yourself up for a successful, profitable outcome. Start your new CDL business today, follow the Clutter Proof System, and run your business the CDL-minded way.

If you found this book to be full of important information for navigating accounting for commercial driving businesses, consider leaving a review on Amazon. This helps more future business owners in the CDL industry set themselves up for long-term success just like you.

Special Bonus Offer: Free Gift for You! :)

CDL Business Productivity
GAME PLAN

Entrepreneurs Guide to Quick Start your Business to the Next Level

Thank you! Here's a Free Gift! For You :)

As a special thanks from me to you, you'll receive:

- ❏ 3 Powerful Elements of Productivity in your Business
- ❏ 5 Simple Strategies to Mastering Productivity in your Business
- ❏ The Highest Quality of Productivity Charts
- ❏ Valuable Resources that you Must Know and much more!

To receive your Free copy of the CDL Business Productivity GAME PLAN, you can go to my website at:
cdlforlife.com/cdl-business-resources

SCAN ME   **SCAN ME**
(For your Free Business Game Plan)   (If you want my Books for Free)

Also If you would like to get my books for Free and before anyone else, go to my website at:
cdlforlife.com/cdl-business-resources

137

REFERENCES

777546. (2015, May 13). *Tracking checks*. Pixabay. https://pixabay.
com/photos/accounting-report-credit-card-761599/

Administration for Children and Families. (2018, Oct. 23). *What's
the difference between an independent contractor and an employee?*
https://www.acf.hhs.gov/css/training-technical-assistance
whats-difference-between-independent-contractor-and-employee

Aymanejed. (2018, Mar. 3). *Business registration*. Pixabay. https://
pixabay.com/photos/laptop-office-hand-writing-3196481/

Barone, A. (2020, Nov. 14). *Factor*. Investopedia. https://www.
investopedia.com/terms/f/factor.asp

Candonga, R. (2020, July 9). *Employee meeting*. Pixabay. https://
pixabay.com/photos/work-office-team-company-internet-
5382501/

Commercial Capital LLC. (n.d.). *Asset based lending vs. factoring*.
https://www.comcapfactoring.com/blog/asset-based-lending-
factoring/

Cpastrick. (2016, June 1). *Log book*. Pixabay. https://pixabay.com/photos/ledger-accounting-business-money-1428230/

Delphinmedia. (2018, Oct. 20). *Tire maintenance*. Pixabay. https://pixabay.com/photos/workshop-aks-measured-track-set-3758513/

Edar. (2015, Sep. 29). *Signing a contract*. Pixabay. https://pixabay.com/photos/business-signature-contract-962355/

Falco. (2014, Nov. 18). *Semi truck on the road*. Pixabay. 1. https://pixabay.com/photos/semi-trailers-truck-road-trailers-534577/

Firmbee. (2015, Jan. 29). *Bookkeeping software*. Pixabay. https://pixabay.com/photos/bookkeeping-accounting-taxes-615384/

Free-Photos. (2016, July 1). *Filling out accounting forms*. Pixabay. https://pixabay.com/photos/office-business-colleagues-meeting-1209640/

Getloaded. (n.d.). *How to start a trucking business*. http://www.getloaded.com/get-authority/how-to-start-a-trucking-business

Great American Insurance. (n.d.). *Occupational accident insurance*. https://www.greatamericaninsurancegroup.com/for-businesses/product-details/trucking/occupational-accident-insurance

Hayashi, R. (2020, Nov. 2). *What are the average credit card processing fees that merchants pay?* Payment Depot. https://paymentdepot.com/blog/average-credit-card-processing-fees/

Iade-Michoko. (2016, Aug. 17). *Fuel pumps*. Pixabay. https://pixabay.com/photos/fuel-pump-energy-gas-pump-1596622/

ImageParty. (2014, Oct. 22). *Odometer*. Pixabay. https://pixabay.com/photos/speedometer-mileage-speed-car-498748/

Internal Revenue Service. (2020, Sep. 29). *How long should I keep records?* https://www.irs.gov/businesses/small-businesses-self-employed/how-long-should-i-keep-records

Kang, S. (2021, Jan. 1). *Computer on a desk*. Pexels. https://www.pexels.com/photo/modern-computer-placed-on-desk-with-lamp-and-radio-in-office-6368911/

Maklay62. (2016, June 1). *Financing cash*. Pixabay. https://pixabay.com/photos/money-dollars-success-business-1428587/

Marcom, H. (2017, May 16). *Budgeting and accounting basics for truckers*. Apex. https://www.apexcapitalcorp.com/blog/budget-accounting-basics-for-truckers/

Murray, J. (2019, Nov. 20). *How to register your business with government entities*. The Balance. https://www.thebalancesmb.com/register-business-federal-entities-397584

Murray, J. (2020, Feb. 28). *Why small businesses need a CPA*. The Balance. https://www.thebalancesmb.com/small-business-cpa-versus-accountant-397384

Muza, C. (2016, Apr. 17). *Accounting software*. Unsplash. https://unsplash.com/photos/hpjSkU2UYSU

Nilov, M. (2021, Feb. 24). *Calculating finances*. Pexels. https://www.pexels.com/photo/man-couple-people-woman-6963847/

Obsahovka, O. (2020, Jan. 14). *Creating a receipt*. Pexels. https://www.pexels.com/photo/wood-businessman-woman-connection-3570239/

PhotoMix-Company. (2020, Nov. 18). *GPS on a phone*. Pixabay. https://pixabay.com/photos/navigation-google-maps-location-5755999/

Roma1880. (2018, Dec. 9). *Organized files*. Pixabay. https://pixabay.com/photos/archive-files-register-office-3859388/

Schneider, D. (2020, Apr. 28). *Comparing cash flow options for your trucking company*. RTS. https://www.rtsinc.com/articles/comparing-cash-flow-options-your-trucking-company

Sikkema, K. (2019, Apr. 2). *Tax forms*. Unsplash. https://unsplash.com/photos/8DEDp6S93Po

Stevepb. (2014, July 9). *Tax registration*. Pixabay. https://pixabay.com/photos/calculator-calculation-insurance-385506/

Tax Policy Center. (2020, May). *Key elements of the U.S. tax system*. https://www.taxpolicycenter.org/briefing-book/how-does-corporate-income-tax-work

Zakhareuski, A. (2021, Mar. 16). *Types of CDL licenses: A, B, and C licenses covered*. Driving Tests. https://driving-tests.org/cdl-classification-licenses/

Thank you for your Honest Experience :)

Thank you! I hope this brings you great value as it did for me sharing my story with you.

My purpose and mission is to guide and encourage you to become the best version of yourself in your life by providing everything you need to achieve your dreams for yourself, your family and your business.

However, in order to do that, sharing your honest review on **amazon** (or Audible) helps spread the word to other CDL Minded friends (like yourself) and will help many readers who are struggling to make their dreams become a reality.

If you do have 30 secs to leave a **1-Click honest review,** I greatly appreciate it because it shows that you're not like most people.

It means that you truly value yourself in what you do. It also means that you're CDL Minded in yourself, your family and in your business.

I truly appreciate all your love and support and I'm thankful and grateful for your life and I greatly value your honest opinion and thoughts. :)

If you need anything, feel free to reach out at my website and to receive your Free Gift if you haven't received it yet.

You can also share your experience by taking a photo of this book and attach it to the review so other CDL Minded friends can be inspired and encouraged from your honest experience.

SCAN ME!

Just One Click (once you click on this review page or scan QR Code):

When you finish, just Click Submit at the bottom of the page and that's it. Please click on this link or scan the QR code to **Review Book on Amazon!**

Overall rating

Add a headline

Add a photo or video

Add a written review

Submit

Looking forward to working together and helping you achieve your goals. Take care and talk to you soon! :)

www.ingramcontent.com/pod-product-compliance
Lightning Source LLC
Chambersburg PA
CBHW031532120626
46545CB00005B/2112